The Shared Kitchen

This book was created and photographed in Meanjin, on the lands of the Turrbal and Jagera peoples. I recognise the enduring connections, kinship and traditions retained in these lands, and I pay my respects to the elders of Turrbal and Jagera Country, past and present. First Nations sovereignty over these lands has never been ceded. This always was and always will be Aboriginal land.

As a white settler on stolen land, I recognise that I am implicated in ongoing processes of colonisation, and that working against this requires tangible action and ultimately, land return.

As a cook and lover of growing and sharing food, I acknowledge the First Nations peoples who have been caring for Country, cooking and sharing sustainably here for tens of thousands of years, and who maintain this connection today.

As an organiser and activist, I turn to First Nations leaders, still being forced to fight for justice on their own land, to resist the ongoing violence of colonisation, and the climate and economic crises it has fuelled. We must all recognise that the solutions to these problems are rooted in self-determination and sovereignty for First Nations peoples.

Fifteen per cent of the author's share from this book will be donated to the Warriors of Aboriginal Resistance and other grassroots First Nations fundraisers and projects in so-called Australia. ✳

The Shared Kitchen
by Clare Scrine

Photography by Yaseera Moosa
Design by Savannah van der Niet
Styling by Issy FitzSimons Reilly

Smith Street Books

Contents

About me

Making and sharing food became an important part of my life when I was ten years old and started to nominate myself for the role of family birthday cake–maker. It was the perfect job for my middle-child sensibilities – a quiet, behind-the-scenes task, but one that, if pulled off right, had the potential to steal a bit of spotlight from my extroverted siblings and wider family.

Two decades later and cooking for me now is more about finding time for calm focus amidst the busyness of everyday life. It's an activity I never seem to tire of, no matter how chaotic or mundane the cooking tasks might be. The process of making food for others, be it a simple dinner with the housemates or a big spread for friends, calms anxiety and gives me a distinct sense of grounding when little else can.

My first book, *The Shared Table*, was supposed to be a little local zine, celebrating the share houses that me and my mates live in, and some dishes I liked to cook. The project grew and grew, and took on a whole life of its own, ending up as a real cookbook distributed across the world. Being able to share some of the joy that cooking brings me with friends and strangers across the planet is pretty damn cool. Any time I heard from someone that my book helped them get back into cooking, or that their share house used it each week to inspire their own house dinners, I'd be filled with a distinct overwhelming feeling of imposter syndrome mixed with a deep sense of joy. When I found myself faced with the fortunate opportunity to write another cookbook, this time the choice was made a lot easier by the thought of all the homes this book might find itself in, and all the people it might help bring together.

So, here it is! Cookbook number two. For those of you who read and enjoyed my first, I do hope this one measures up. And for those who've stumbled on it another way, I hope these recipes and snapshots of share-house life inspire some tasty meals, great conversations and perhaps a few moments of quiet contentment. *

About The Shared Kitchen

The idea for this book came to me when I was on 'fridge-and-pantry duty' in my share house, which involves the sometimes (read: often) gross task of clearing out our communal veggie crisper of its too-far-gone vegetables – one of the joys of sharing a kitchen in a big, busy, share house! This particular week I threw out almost an entire kilo of carrots that had been there a week or two too long for even my 'cut off the mould, she'll be right' approach to produce. It got me thinking about how tricky it can be to find inspiration for a meal from our most common ingredients. That bag of carrots could have been used in a million ways instead of ending up in our compost bin.

So one aspect of this book is about reducing waste, saving those precious fresh ingredients from the bin. But it's also about the pleasure and therapeutic joy of cooking with what you already have — whether that was grown in your garden, discovered at the bottom of a slightly gross veggie crisper, or sold in cheap buckets at the market. It's always nice turning something simple into something special, and this book is born from that.

In these pages you'll find 16 chapters, each containing a generous handful of recipes that feature one fruit or veg as their centrepiece. The fruits and vegetables in this book were chosen for their general availability and affordability. For many of us these foods are basic staples – apples, potatoes, onions, zucchini (courgettes) and so on. They're the humble fruits and vegetables we might buy in bulk, but then struggle to find inspiration to cook with in new or enjoyable ways.

The recipes here are plentiful and packed with flavour, but mostly still simple enough for beginner cooks. They endeavour to provide you with fresh ideas for what to make, as well as offering some fun, unfamiliar flavour combinations. Of course, there are plenty of classic here too. The recipes have also been tested by a raft of friends and acquaintances to ensure their cookability and tastiness, and I've included a comprehensive ingredient swap list on page 18, which will hopefully encourage you to cook from what you already have as much as possible.

The recipes are also all vegetarian, with about half of them vegan, while many more can be veganised using the suggested ingredients swaps. I'm conscious of moralising about individual food consumption and its effect on the world. They say vegetarianism reduces your 'carbon footprint', but that term was invented by a PR team working for British Petroleum in 2004. Let's not get caught in the spin that transfers blame from powerful, profit-seeking mega-polluters to regular people living under capitalism. Still, cow burps and mass-clearing of trees for cattle aren't exactly cooling the planet, so I do cook vegetarian for the bit of difference it can make, and the fun challenge that making meals from vegetables brings. You don't need meat to make great meals.

Like my first book, *The Shared Kitchen* invites you into share houses around my home city of Meanjin in Brisbane, Australia. The recipes were all created in a sometimes-chaotic shared kitchen in my own home, and in these pages we have the pleasure of visiting other shared kitchens around the city. I'm so grateful to all the people who invited us in to capture a little slice of their lives. I have always loved living communally, and hope to continue doing so, maybe forever (hello, housing crisis). Affordability aside, sharing a home with friends who become family, and strangers who become friends, has undoubtedly been the greates gift of my twenties. ✳

About how cooked it all is ...

Like everything, food, cooking and eating are inherently political. I'm deeply conscious of the world I experience as an able-bodied, educated, white cis-woman in so-called Australia. The choice to take a few months off paid work to write a cookbook is an incredible privilege, and the opportunity to have it published widely isn't one I view lightly. Hell, even having the time, resources and energy to think about what one eats every day is a product of immense fortune.

Even here, in so-called Australia, there are communities that cannot access the fruits and vegetables that make up these chapters. Accessing seasonal produce cheaply is a privilege that is not possible for many regional and remote communities, in particular First Nations communities. For people forced to live in poverty because of inadequate government support and a jobs shortage, the option to eat and cook fresh food is often not realistic. It goes without saying that healthy, good food should not be a luxury and in a country as rich as this one we can afford to ensure no one goes hungry.

The pandemic has only further highlighted the sheer depths of inequality and inequity that rots our society from every direction. As its waves continue, we have seen the fragility of food systems under capitalism laid bare. For the first time for many of us, we've seen emptied supermarket shelves and severe shortages of basic supplies, from fresh fruit and vegetables to tinned goods and toilet paper. This should serve as a stark reminder to us all what food insecurity might look like, as we face an uncertain economic and environmental future. Like most of the impacts of climate catastrophe, it's the communities already facing marginalisation and disadvantage who will face these food shortages first and hardest. They already are.

We need radical solutions to challenge injustice and tackle the environmental issues that will loom ever larger this decade. We need to reimagine our society and organise collectively towards transformational change that does more than tinker around the edges. Part of that work must include rethinking our food sources, systems and relationships. It is crucial that we change how we relate to one another, how we build and maintain communities outside of capitalism that are centred on mutual aid and community networks, both as a tool to get us to that place of transformation, and a way to stay sane while we do it.

One of the most inspiring projects that has come out of my home town in recent years is a bunch of guerilla gardens, created under the banner of 'Growing Forward'. The first garden was established as Meanjin went into lockdown at the start of the pandemic. It was a direct response to bare supermarket shelves and inadequate government support for a casualised workforce, that sparked a welcome surge in local mutual-aid projects. The Growing Forward gardens mobilise volunteers to take over under-used empty land and turn it into thriving urban farms. The abundance of produce they grow and harvest is given away for free to communities in need.

Some of the problems I've mentioned (and many more I'm sure you're aware of) are just so big they feel unfixable. But we mustn't let despair take hold. If you can, join or start your own community garden, get politically active, volunteer, take direct action and join and participate in your local community groups. There's just so much to do, and I promise you'll make the best friends along the way. If you don't feel like you have the skills and experience to offer much, but you're simply reading this book because you love food and cooking, perhaps find a grassroots group whose work you connect with and reach out and offer to cook for their members or cater their next event. Connect with a local group providing mutual aid and community care and help them cook and provide meals to people who need them. Introduce yourself to your neighbours, share your leftovers and drop people you love home-cooked meals.

The work of saving this planet and tackling injustice is tough but there's so many amazing people to meet and delicious meals to share along the way. ✱

Cooking notes

When basing your meals around vegetables, building in flavour can require a bit more creativity and time than if you are cooking with meat. Here are a few notes – or general principles – for how these recipes achieve that, and how you can take your everyday cooking up a notch.

Seasoning

I tend to use flaky sea salt in most of my savoury cooking, though for baked goods, breads and doughs it is absolutely fine to use table salt, which is what I've used for most of the measurements here. If you're subbing in flaky salt, ensure you up the quantity and, of course, taste to check. Don't be afraid of using salt liberally, it's essential for tasty food, including in baked goods. Season and taste dishes as you go, building seasoning into each stage and layer of a meal. As you give something a final taste before serving, consider if it needs an extra pinch of salt or glug of olive oil. There are few dishes that can't be enhanced by these ingredients. As for pepper, freshly cracked black or ground white pepper are my general go-tos, each providing depth and warmth, well suited to different cuisines.

Vegetable stock

I use a lot of vegetable stock in my recipes, and I generally believe there's nothing wrong with using stock cubes or liquid stock. However, getting into the habit of saving your vegetable scraps and boiling them up in a pot every few weeks to use in meals is a nice ritual that ensures you always have some really beautiful stuff in the fridge or freezer at the ready, plus it makes use of your off-cuts. Make sure to always include some aromatics in your stockpot too, such as lemon, peppercorns, whole spices, herbs, bay leaves or chilli. Don't salt stock until the end, and ensure that you cook it long enough (at least an hour or two).

Stop wasting liquid!

There's so much flavour packed into the liquid of your tinned beans, pickles, cheeses, olives and more. Use it in salad dressings, sauces or marinades in place of vinegar or oil. The whey from cheese and the soaking liquid from beans are flavourful and packed with good stuff. Simply add a splash to whatever you're cooking, or swap out water or stock.

Love your leftovers

A lot of food tastes better the next day. When you grow sick of eating
something, try to think about how you can transform it into something new.
A cake can become a tiramisu or a trifle; your tomato pasta sauce can become
host to baked eggs or thickened and sweetened a little into a chutney; tomato
salad leftovers can be cooked into a pasta sauce; roasted vegetable-based
salads can become pie or frittata fillings; and leftover dips double up brilliantly
as the base for delicious toasted sandwiches or salad bowls.

Don't feel beholden to a recipe

The best food inventions came from failures. Cooking from a recipe book
(in my opinion) is less about a strict set of instructions and more about
finding inspiration and new ideas to expand your repertoire. Baking sweets
can be more finicky, but if something goes wrong it's often salvageable, so try
searching for a fix online to enrich your understanding of the food science
behind the ingredients you're using. Use these recipes as a starting point, but
spend more time tasting and thinking about the food in front of you than the
words on the page.

Grow some stuff

You don't need a thriving urban farm in your backyard to try your hand at homegrown produce. Even a few big pots filled with seasonal herbs, leafy greens and
chillies will save you cash, and let you enhance meals easily with pops of flavour.
I only got into gardening in a semi-serious way in the last few years, but it has
improved my quality of life significantly. Getting your hands in the soil, watching
hard work pay off as things grow, and being able to thrust some fresh produce
into friends' hands when they come to visit is all good stuff.

Gear and ingredients

There are a couple of kitchen gadgets I rely on heavily: a large food processor
with grating and slicing attachments; a high-powered blender or stick blender
for making silky sauces; and electric beaters (I don't bother with a stand mixer).
Nowadays you can buy gadgets that essentially contain all three functions.
If you're not into cooking in a serious way you can survive without them, but
I do use them a fair bit throughout these recipes.

As for ingredients, it's all been said before but having a well-stocked pantry
does make cooking cheaper and more enjoyable. I don't think any of these
recipes use ingredients that most people won't have heard of; they're designed
to be whipped up on a whim from a well-stocked fridge and pantry as that's
how I like to cook. ✱

Ingredients swaps

I've always aspired to be the kind of cook who can make something special out of whatever lies in the back of the pantry, mixed with whatever scraps need using up in the kitchen. Part of being able to do that, is knowing what ingredients can be easily substituted with something else, for largely the same outcome.

So here are some substitution options for the more common ingredients in this book. Recipes with vegan or gluten-free options, or more novel ingredients, have suggested substitutes on their recipe page. However, I encourage you to think of this list as a starting point, rather than a definitive guide. Whenever I swap an ingredient in a dish, I ask myself: what is this ingredient providing? What else can do that job? Richness? Sweetness? Depth of flavour? What kind of flavour?

Despite what some cooks or food writers will tell you, recipes generally won't crumble and fail if you swap out even the most central ingredient. The next time you think you need to run out to buy more stuff just to make a dish, pause and think, can I use an ingredient I already have? You might even discover a new, delicious flavour combination.

Allspice	mixed spice or an equal mixture of ground nutmeg and cloves
Almonds	walnuts, pistachios, pumpkin seeds (pepitas) or sunflower seeds
Apple cider vinegar	rice wine–based vinegar or white wine vinegar
Balsamic vinegar	wine-based vinegar or apple cider vinegar
Basil	mint, parsley, dill or fennel leaves
Brown sugar	5:1 caster (superfine) sugar with honey, golden syrup or maple syrup
Buffalo mozzarella	soft goat's cheese, feta or haloumi
Burrata	fresh mozzarella, soft feta or goat's cheese
Butter (lima) beans	cannellini beans or chickpeas (garbanzo beans)
Capers	green olives
Cardamom pods	whole cloves or 1 teaspoon ground cardamom, allspice or mixed spice
Cashews	almonds, sunflower seeds, macadamia nuts, pine nuts or walnuts
Cayenne pepper	chilli powder or fresh chilli
Chickpeas (garbanzo beans)	butter (lima) beans, cannellini beans or borlotti beans

Chilli	chilli flakes or chopped pickled jalapenos
Chinese five spice	DIY mix of star anise, fennel seeds, cinnamon, peppercorns and cloves (or as many of these as you have, plus some ground cumin), bashed using a mortar and pestle
Coconut cream	coconut milk, plus 1 tablespoon of tahini for thickness and richness
Coriander (cilantro)	mint or parsley or a combination of both
Cornflour (corn starch)	plain (all-purpose) flour
Cream	sour cream, crème fraîche or cream cheese
Cream cheese	mascarpone, cream or extra milk
Crème fraîche	sour cream or thickened cream
Currants	cranberries, sultanas (golden raisins) or roughly chopped raisins or dried apricots
Dates	raisins, sultanas (golden raisins) or dried apricots
Dill	mint, parsley or oregano
Dijon mustard	another mustard or mustard powder
Dried mushrooms	200 g (7 oz) fresh plus 500 ml (2 cups) vegetable stock
Fennel seeds	caraway seeds or 2 teaspoons garam masala
Garlic powder	fresh garlic
Golden syrup	honey or maple syrup
Green chilli	1–2 tablespoons chopped pickled jalapenos, chilli powder or chilli sauce
Ground ginger	ground cardamom
Harissa	tomato paste (concentrated purée) mixed with a little chilli powder, ground cumin, paprika and vinegar
Honey	maple syrup or brown sugar
Leek	fennel, shallots, spring onions (scallions), brown onion or brussels sprouts
Lemon juice	lime juice, apple cider vinegar or wine-based vinegar
Lemon zest	other citrus zest
Lentils	black beans, kidney beans, borlotti beans or navy beans
Lime juice	lemon juice, apple cider vinegar or wine-based vinegar

Lime zest	lemon zest
Liquid smoke	for each teaspoon, substitute 1 teaspoon balsamic vinegar plus 1 teaspoon smoky paprika
Maple syrup	honey
Mascarpone	cream cheese
Mint	dill, basil or flat-leaf parsley
Miso paste	soy sauce
Nutmeg	allspice or ground cinnamon
Nutritional yeast	grated parmesan, vegan cheese or seasoned breadcrumbs
Onion	leek, celery or spring onions (scallions)
Oregano	thyme, rosemary or tarragon
Parmesan	soft feta or goat's cheese
Parsley	basil, dill or mint (or a mix)
Pecans	any other nuts, fennel or cumin seeds
Pine nuts	blanched almonds or walnuts
Pistachios	any other nuts or pumpkin seeds (pepitas)
Pumpkin seeds (pepitas)	sunflower seeds or any nuts, roughly chopped
Radishes	red onion or spring onions (scallions)
Red onion	caramelised brown onion, spring onions (scallions) or radishes
Red wine vinegar	white wine vinegar or apple cider vinegar
Rice	quinoa, pearl barley or pearl couscous, adjusting liquid and cooking time as required
Rosemary	thyme
Sage	rosemary, tarragon, thyme or oregano
Seeded (wholegrain) mustard	English mustard or dijon mustard
Sesame seeds	chopped peanuts or crispy fried shallots
Sour cream	natural yoghurt, cream, mascarpone, crème fraîche or milk with a squeeze of lemon juice
Spring onions (scallions)	chives, parsley stalks or 1 brown onion, sliced and cooked in olive oil for 5 minutes
Sultanas (golden raisins)	currants, raisins or chopped dates
Sumac	1:1 lemon zest and paprika
Tahini	sesame oil in savoury dishes, almond or peanut butter in sweet
Thyme	tarragon, oregano or dill
Tomato ketchup	barbecue sauce or any chutney/relish you have open
Tomato passata	chopped fresh tomatoes or crushed tinned tomatoes
Tomato paste	100 g (3½ oz) tomato passata (puréed tomatoes)
Tomatoes (fresh)	tomato passata (puréed tomatoes) or crushed tinned tomatoes
Walnuts	almonds, pumpkin seeds (pepitas) or sunflower seeds
White wine vinegar	lemon juice
Yoghurt	sour cream or buttermilk. *

Apple

Recipes

When I was a kid, I threw out the apple that was packed in my lunchbox every day for about 10 years (sorry, Mum). The thought now obviously makes me feel deeply uncomfortable; I'm not sure why I never told anyone I hated them. For many of us, apples do have a certain sense of being ever-present, the eternal packed-lunch snack. Of course I love them now, especially with spices and creamy ingredients in desserts. Apples are also most welcome in savoury dishes too; their acidity and sharp crunch a perfect addition.

With Hayley, Greg, Mel, Lachie, Bri and Gareth

Describe your household

We are six young people living in an inner-city farmhouse complete with holes in the floor, mice in the larder and chickens clucking at dawn and dusk. In fact, you can see the city's skyscrapers from the henhouse.

The house itself is older and has more stories in its walls than the sum of ages of all its inhabitants. We love our home because it is a spot to escape from what goes on in our careers and our lives away from the house. We all work in the realm of politics and ecology, so having a home overrun with vines and wild plants seems to fit in the picture nicely.

Do you share food as a household? How often and what does that involve?

We share food more for pleasure than practicality. Breakfast, lunch and dinner can be fragmented and staggered, where we eat at different times from different drawers. But we come together often, sometimes for a Sunday breakfast, complete with hash browns and orange juice, or a dinner of homemade pasta, paired with the wine we happen to have above the fridge. Sometimes our lives get in the way but our favourite place to come together is always over a home-cooked meal.

How do you navigate sharing a kitchen?

There are very few rules, and no rosters in our household, but there is a lot of common understanding that comes from living together for a long time.

The most challenging thing is keeping the fridge organised. We are all guilty of abandoning leftovers in the darkest, most furry corners, and every once in a while we have to own up to mouldy Tupperware and conduct the walk of shame to the compost bin.

We also have to keep all of our food under lock and key because our house is basically a wildlife corridor. We have resident possums, rats that we name and get emotionally attached to, and neighbourhood cats that come to stalk the rats. Leave food out and you will wake up to nibbled debris on the kitchen floor.

What's your favourite way to cook or eat apples?

Apple pie. There is little more satisfying than the cross-hatched, swollen pastry steaming on the kitchen bench.

What do you love most about your share house?

Our house has been a rolling share house for so long that we can't account for half of what's in it. It seems to breed furniture (and mice).

We think that because of this, the house has a certain kind of magic greater than the sum of the people currently living there. We have had people knock on our door who lived here five to 10 years ago, wanting to check on the trees they planted or to see whether old friends were still around.

The joy of living in a share house like ours is never being lonely, especially when the walls are as thin as ours. The company more than makes up for the eternally mouldy shower or a housemate's habit of abandoning laundry on the clothesline. *

Grated tofu & apple tacos with avocado cream

Serves 4–6 · Vegan · Gluten Free

½ tsp salt

2 tsp ground cumin

2 tsp ground coriander

1 tsp smoky paprika

1 tsp garlic powder

1 tsp dried oregano

500 g (1 lb 2 oz) extra-firm tofu, grated

2 tbsp olive oil

250 g (1 cup) passata (puréed tomatoes)

2 tsp liquid smoke

60 ml (¼ cup) barbecue sauce

2 tsp hot sauce of your choice

Apple slaw

2 tbsp apple cider vinegar

1 garlic clove, finely minced or grated

zest and juice of 1 lime

1½ tbsp caster (superfine) sugar

½ tsp salt

3–4 large apples, cored, grated using a box grater

½ bunch of coriander (cilantro), stems and leaves chopped

½ red onion, grated

Apples provide a super delicious and fresh hit of flavour and crunch to these tacos, and complement the spiced baked tofu really nicely. It's tossed in a strong pickle-like dressing which squarely transfers the sweet apple flavour into savoury territory. It is crucial to use extra-firm tofu (or regular firm at a pinch) or you'll have trouble grating it. If you think your tofu is too wet, wrap it in a clean tea towel and weigh it down with a chopping board or heavy book for 30 minutes, to remove some of the excess water before grating.

Preheat the oven to 180°C (350°F) fan-forced and line a large baking tray with baking paper.

In a small bowl, combine the salt, ground spices and dried oregano. Spread the grated tofu onto the prepared tray, then sprinkle over the spice mix and add the olive oil. Use your hands or some tongs to toss the tofu a little and roughly coat it in the mix. Transfer to the oven and bake for 15–20 minutes, until the tofu strands are beginning to brown a little.

Meanwhile, whisk the passata, liquid smoke, barbecue sauce and hot sauce in a bowl. Remove the tofu from the oven and pour over the passata mixture, using your tongs to roughly toss the mixture through the tofu. Return the tray to the oven and bake for a further 15 minutes or until the tofu is golden and sticky.

While the tofu cooks, prepare the apple slaw by whisking together the vinegar, garlic, lime zest and juice, caster sugar and salt in a bowl. Add the apple, coriander and onion and toss well. Set aside until ready to serve.

To make the avocado cream, blend all the ingredients in a high-powered blender, adding a little water, if necessary, to get things moving. Taste and add extra salt, pepper or lime juice to your liking. Pour the cream into a bowl and set aside.

Just before the tofu is ready, wrap the tortillas in foil or cover in a baking dish and warm them through in the oven.

Take everything to the table and serve with extra coriander leaves and chopped pickled jalapeno, if you like. ✳

<u>Avocado cream</u>

2 avocados, flesh scooped out

2 tbsp olive oil

½ tsp salt

pinch of pepper

1 garlic clove, peeled

2 tbsp white wine vinegar

60 ml (¼ cup) milk of your choice

1 tbsp lime juice, plus extra if needed

<u>To serve</u>

12–16 corn or flour tortillas

coriander (cilantro) leaves

chopped pickled jalapenos (optional)

Swaps

Apple – shredded cabbage, kohlrabi, fennel or radish

Tofu – tempeh, shredded plant-based chicken or mince

Luxe potato, apple & fennel bake

Serves 4–6, or 8–10 as a side

4 potatoes, peeled

2 large apples, peeled and cored (I use Granny Smith but any tart variety is fine)

1 small fennel bulb (or ½ large bulb)

75 g (2¾ oz) salted butter

35 g (¼ cup) plain (all-purpose) flour

625 ml (2½ cups) milk

220 g (1 cup) mascarpone

1 tbsp wholegrain mustard

1 tsp dried thyme (or 1 tbsp fresh leaves)

salt and pepper

200 g (2 cups) grated cheese (I use a mix of cheddar, parmesan and gouda, but any combination will work)

1½ tbsp white wine vinegar, plus extra if needed

50 g (½ cup) pecans, chopped

small handful of fresh thyme, oregano or sage leaves (optional)

Swaps

Gluten free – plain flour: cornflour (corn starch) or potato starch

Vegan – butter: olive oil (skip the browning step); milk: plant-based milk; mascarpone: plant-based milk or a mix of 200 ml (7 fl oz) plant-based milk and 2 tbsp cashew cheese; cheese: nutritional yeast or vegan cheese

Fennel – leek, zucchini, brussels sprouts, onion, Jerusalem artichoke or kohlrabi

Mascarpone – sour cream, double-thickened (dollop) cream or cashew cream

This is a seriously turbo-charged potato bake, with plenty of fun additions to wow your housemates or dinner companions. Apple slices add a slightly unexpected but super-moreish note of sweetness, while the browned butter, wholegrain mustard, mascarpone and thyme give the dish much more flavour than your standard potato bake. I also love how easy it is to make – no pre-cooking of the veggies is required, just slice them super thin, make the sauce, combine and bake. Serve alongside some veggie sausages and a salad for a great dinner, or take this bake along to your next potluck.

Preheat the oven to 200°C (400°F) fan-forced.

Using a mandoline or a sharp knife, slice the potatoes, apples and fennel into paper-thin slices (1 mm/¹⁄₁₆ in or thinner). This can also be done very efficiently using the blade attachment of a food processor. Transfer the sliced veggies and apple to a large baking dish and toss them together to combine well.

Melt the butter in a saucepan over medium heat. Cook the butter until it sizzles, and eventually foams up and begins to smell nutty and turn brown in parts. This will take a few minutes and it's important to watch closely so it doesn't burn. When it has browned, add the flour and whisk well to combine, forming a silky roux that looks like caramel. Continue to whisk for 1 minute to cook the flour a little, then slowly pour in the milk, whisking as you go to help prevent the sauce becoming lumpy. Continue whisking for 2–3 minutes, until the sauce has thickened considerably. Add 250 ml (1 cup) of water, the mascarpone, mustard, thyme and a generous pinch or two of salt and pepper, then stir well to incorporate all the ingredients. Cook until the sauce starts to simmer, then turn off the heat, add two-thirds of the cheese and stir until it has melted into the sauce. Add the vinegar, which adds a nice touch of sharpness to the creamy mix, then taste and add extra seasoning or vinegar to your liking.

Pour the sauce over the vegetables and apple in the baking dish and, using tongs, gently toss to coat them in the thick, cheesy sauce until completely covered on all sides. Wipe away any sauce from the outside of the baking dish, and cover it with foil. Transfer the dish to the oven and bake for 45 minutes or until the veggies and apple are slightly tender when poked with a fork. Remove the dish from the oven and take off the foil. Sprinkle the remaining cheese over the top, then scatter with the chopped pecans and fresh herbs (if using). Return to the oven for an additional 15–20 minutes, until the cheese is melted and golden. Let the bake cool for 5–10 minutes before serving. *

Apple & almond cake with caramel cream

Makes 1 x 20 cm (8 in) cake

150 g (5½ oz) unsalted butter, softened

140 g (¾ cup) brown sugar

1 tsp vanilla extract

3 eggs

2 tsp apple cider vinegar

125 ml (½ cup) milk

½ tsp ground ginger

1 tsp ground cinnamon

¼ tsp salt

1½ tsp bicarbonate of soda (baking soda)

300 g (2 cups) self-raising flour

120 g (1 cup) almond meal (ideally chopped/blitzed yourself with some larger chunks)

4 apples (skin on), grated

Caramel cream icing

115 g (½ cup) brown sugar

100 g (3½ oz) butter

375 ml (1½ cups) thickened cream

pinch of flaky sea salt

125 g (1 cup) icing (confectioners') sugar

Swaps

Gluten free – self-raising flour: gluten-free self-raising flour

Vegan – butter: vegan margarine or vegetable oil; eggs: 1 mashed banana or 3 chia/flax eggs; milk: plant-based milk; omit the icing, or replace with your favourite vegan caramel icing.

Apples – pears

This apple cake is so delightfully moist and easy to make. Though it contains heaps of apple, it's grated and mostly acts as a moisture agent, much in the same way that carrot does in carrot cake. The caramel cream icing takes it to another level, but you could leave it out and make this as a loaf cake, served with butter. I like using homemade almond meal, from chopped or blitzed whole almonds, so there's a fair bit more texture, but the packet stuff works great too.

In a large mixing bowl, beat or whisk the soft butter and brown sugar until light and fluffy. Add the vanilla extract, then beat in the eggs one at a time. Add the vinegar and milk and stir through.

In a separate bowl whisk the spices, salt, bicarbonate of soda, flour and almond meal until well combined. Tip the flour mixture into the wet ingredients and stir to form a shaggy, thick cake batter. Add the grated apple and gently fold it all together with a spoon, until the apple is well distributed. Set the mixture aside for 10–15 minutes. During this time juice will seep out of the apple and moisten the cake batter, ensuring a beautiful crumb in your cake.

While you wait, preheat the oven to 180°C (350°F) fan-forced and line the base and sides of two (ideally springform) 20 cm (8 in) cake tins with baking paper, or grease them well with butter. If you prefer, you can also make a single, large cake in a 25–30 cm (10–12 in) cake or loaf tin.

Pour the cake batter into the tins and spread it out using the back of a spoon or a pastry scraper so it's even. Transfer the tins to the oven and bake the cakes for 30–35 minutes (45–50 minutes if making one large cake), until they are just set and a skewer comes out mostly clean. Leave the cakes to cool for 10 minutes, then release them from the tins and cool completely on wire racks.

Meanwhile, prepare the caramel cream icing. Melt the brown sugar and butter in a small saucepan over medium–low heat, stirring often, until the sugar has dissolved completely. Increase the heat to medium–high and bring the mixture to the boil and cook, without stirring, for 2–3 minutes. During this time, the mixture will bubble and darken to an amber brown, and begin to smell like caramel. Remove from the heat and whisk in 125 ml (½ cup) of the cream and the salt, and stir until well combined. Leave the mix to cool completely.

Once the caramel is cool, use electric beaters to beat in the icing sugar and remaining cream on low speed, until the icing forms soft peaks.

Once the cake is completely cooled, place one cake on your serving plate and top with about half the icing, spreading it across the top of the cake to create a thick filling. Place the second cake on top (if it has a significant curve on top, sometimes I place it upside down to get a nice flat top). Top with the remaining icing, swirling it on top, and around the sides too, if you like. Decorate with any toppings you fancy and serve fresh. Any leftovers will keep, covered, in the fridge for a day or two. *

Old-school apple custard pull-apart

Makes 1 large pull-apart (Serves 6–8)

125 ml (½ cup) milk, lukewarm

½ tsp instant dried yeast

3 tbsp caster (superfine) sugar

1 egg

50 g (1¾ oz) salted butter, melted

1 tsp vanilla essence

½ tsp ground cinnamon

300 g (2 cups) plain (all-purpose) flour, plus extra if needed and for dusting

½ tsp salt

Apple filling

3 apples (about 500 g/1 lb 2 oz), peeled, cored and cut into 1 cm (½ in) cubes

25 g (¾ oz) salted butter

2 tsp lemon juice

½ tsp ground cinnamon

Custard

250 ml (1 cup) milk

1 tsp vanilla essence

1 heaped tbsp cornflour (corn starch)

3 tbsp caster (superfine) sugar

2 egg yolks

1 whole egg

pinch of salt

Inspired by my favourite cheap bakery snack, this brioche pull-apart makes for a brilliant morning or afternoon tea. Gently cooked apples that are still firm are packed in around perfectly creamy, but not-too-goopy, homemade custard, and encased in a soft brioche dough. You could make all sorts of additions or adjustments to this dish, subbing in other fruit like pears or stone fruit, or adding berries, rhubarb or sultanas. If you want to simplify or speed up this recipe, use thick pre-made custard and a large tin of stewed apples.

Whisk the warm milk, yeast and sugar in a bowl and set aside for 10 minutes until foamy.

Meanwhile, to make the apple filling, combine the ingredients in a small saucepan and heat over medium heat. Once the butter has melted, stir the apples well to coat, then cover with a lid and leave the apple to cook gently for about 5 minutes until softened. Remove the pan from the heat and allow the apple mixture to cool completely.

Add the egg, melted butter, vanilla and cinnamon to the milk mixture and whisk until well combined. Add the flour and salt and whisk well to evenly distribute. Use your hands, lightly dusted with flour, to bring the mixture into a ball and knead for 5 minutes on your work surface. The dough will feel quite sticky but shouldn't stick to your hands. Add a little extra flour if it does. The dough is ready once it becomes very soft and pliable. Return to the bowl, cover with a tea towel and leave to rise in a warm spot for 30–60 minutes.

While the dough rises, prepare the custard. Place the milk and vanilla in a saucepan and warm over low heat until it starts to simmer. In a separate bowl, whisk the remaining custard ingredients together until smooth. Once the milk is almost boiling, remove it from the heat and gently pour it into the egg mixture in a slow, steady stream, whisking constantly. The custard should look frothy. Pour the mixture back into the pan and set over medium–low heat. Whisk the custard constantly for 2–3 minutes, until it becomes thick and glossy. The exact time this will take depends upon the size of your pan and the heat, but it's important to keep a close eye on it. Continue to whisk until the custard is nice and thick, then remove from the heat and set aside to cool.

Once the dough has close to doubled in size, preheat the oven to 200°C (400°F) fan-forced and line a 25 x 35 cm (10 x 14 in) baking tray with baking paper. Gently tip the dough out onto a clean, lightly floured work surface. Split the dough into two portions, one about double the size of the other. Roll the larger ball of dough into an oval, about 30 cm (12 in) long and 25 cm (10 in) wide at the widest point. Carefully transfer the dough to the prepared tray by rolling it up onto your rolling pin, then unrolling it onto the tray.

Scoop more than half of the apple filling onto the dough and spread it out, leaving a 5 cm (2 in) border. Spoon the cooled custard over the top, then finish with the remaining apple filling.

Topping

1 egg, whisked

handful of flaked almonds

85 g (⅔ cup) icing (confectioners') sugar

2 tbsp milk

pinch of salt

Swaps

Apples – pears, stone fruit or berries

Milk and butter – plant-based alternatives

Roll the remaining ball of dough into a long strip, then arrange it over the filling in a zig-zag pattern, or divide it into one long strip and 6–8 smaller strips, and use them to create a leaf pattern. Fold the dough border onto itself, pressing it with a fork or folding it all around the edges like a galette. Brush the dough with the whisked egg, then scatter over the almonds. Bake for 20–25 minutes, until puffy and golden brown.

As it cooks, prepare a simple icing by whisking the icing sugar, milk and a pinch of salt to form a thick glossy mix. Allow the brioche to cool a little, then drizzle the icing over the top. The pull-apart is great warm or cold and will keep, wrapped in the fridge, for up to 2 days. ✳

Rustic apple pie

Serves 8–10 · Vegan

375 g (2½ cups) plain (all-purpose) flour, plus extra if needed and for dusting

2 tbsp caster (superfine) sugar, plus extra for sprinkling

1 tsp salt

100 g (about ½ cup) refrigerated coconut oil

170 ml (⅔ cup) ice-cold water, plus extra if needed

2 tbsp milk of your choice

ice cream or cream of your choice, to serve (optional)

Apple pie filling

2 tbsp cornflour (corn starch)

115 g (½ cup) brown sugar

1 tbsp lemon juice

2 tsp ground cinnamon

½ tsp ground ginger

2 tsp vanilla essence

6 large apples, peeled, cored and sliced into thin wedges (about 2 mm/⅛ in thick)

Swaps

Apples – pears, stone fruit, rhubarb or berries

Coconut oil – butter

This is the first time I've made vegan pastry that genuinely competes with all-butter pastry. In fact, I am willing to say you might not even pick it's vegan. Coconut oil, with a few key tricks, disperses through the flour in a very similar way to butter, and when kept cold by using iced water and working quickly, it creates an amazingly crispy and flaky crumb. The filling is super simple, but perfectly tart and flavoursome. You could get creative and add stewed rhubarb or other fruits, such as pears, berries or stone fruit, or mix up the spices.

Combine the flour, sugar and salt in a mixing bowl. Chop the cold coconut oil into small pieces, then add it to the flour mixture. Use a fork, scissors or a sharp knife to 'cut' through the mixture repeatedly, slicing the oil into tinier pieces and dispersing it through the flour in the process. After a minute or two you'll have a breadcrumb-like consistency, with most of the oil broken up. If you need to, you can also use your fingertips to rub the coconut oil through the flour, but you'll need to work quickly so the heat from your fingers doesn't melt the oil. Pour in the ice-cold water, then use a fork or spoon to mix the water through the flour mixture to form a sticky, shaggy dough. Use your hands to bring the dough together into a ball, adding a little extra flour or water if needed. Wrap the dough or place in a bowl covered with a plate and set aside in the fridge to rest for at least 10 minutes (up to overnight) to firm up.

Preheat the oven to 180°C (350°F) fan-forced and grease or line a pie tin or baking tray with baking paper.

To make the apple pie filling, combine the ingredients, except the apple, in a bowl. Add the apple and toss well to coat, then set aside.

Remove the pastry from the fridge and divide it into two pieces, one slightly bigger than the other. On a lightly floured work surface, roll each piece of dough into a rough circular disc, about 3–4 mm (³⁄₁₆ in) thick and 20–25 cm (8–10 in) wide. Transfer the larger disc to the prepared pie tin or baking tray (rolling it carefully onto the rolling pin, then unrolling it over the tin or tray is the easiest way to do this without breakages; if the pastry does tear as you roll it out or try to move it, just patch it back up).

Scoop the apple filling onto the pastry (leave a 1 cm/½ in border if baking the pie on a baking tray). Drizzle any juices that have collected in the bowl over the top of the apple, then gently place the remaining disc of pastry over the top. To seal the pie, you can either scallop the edges by folding them over and onto themselves or use a fork to press down and create a crimped edge. Brush the milk over the pastry and sprinkle with 2 teaspoons of sugar. Use a sharp knife to cut a small hole in the middle of the pastry, to allow steam to escape as the pie cooks.

Transfer the pie to the oven and bake for 30–40 minutes, until golden brown. Serve warm with ice cream or cream, if you like. The leftovers will keep well in an airtight container in the fridge for a couple of days. ✳

Banana

Most of us rely on a good banana bread or cake as a staple in our baking repertoire, and they're a classic for a reason. Bananas are also a great vegan egg substitute in lots of baked goods and are perfectly used this way when over-ripe (and frozen). For a long time these were the only way I'd use bananas, save for an occasional smoothie or on some peanut butter toast. Writing this book gave me the motivation to go a bit deeper, and the humble banana has a reboot here with some knock-out desserts that are sure to impress a crowd. Their subtle, creamy flavour makes for a lovely pairing with chocolate, caramel and even miso.

With Clare, Isy, Maeve, Fynn and Isha

Describe your household

We are five people who all do pretty different stuff and live together harmoniously. Maeve teaches small humans and draws houses, Fynn works in a university and plays A LOT of frisbee, Isy makes art and studies archiving, Isha makes music, sells bikes and wanders around the house aimlessly, and you've heard enough about Clare.

How do you navigate sharing food and a kitchen?

We are lucky to have a big kitchen in this house – it makes busy dinnertimes easy. We have a communal pantry and fridge, and a decent veggie garden, so there's always stuff to cook and eat. We try to keep things nice and relatively clean with a not-too-uptight-but-keeps-the-peace jobs roster.

We do share food, mostly when Clare cooks for everyone. Sometimes she goes away, and we forget how to cook and everyone eats toast for a week. Most of us do like cooking though – Maeve tests Clare's recipes a lot, and Clare tries not to micromanage. Issy specialises in one-pot delights and Isha does wild things to a can of baked beans. Fynn, well not so much, she only turned on the oven for the first time last week, but she's a crucial part of the ecosystem because she eats all our leftovers.

What's your favourite way to cook/eat bananas?

Maeve likes bananas super ripe, then frozen for her daily smoothie before school, generally at an unspeakably early hour in the morning. Isha thinks banana Nesquik is banana at its best. Isy hates banana and feels ripped off that this was our allocated chapter. Fynn loves bananas because they involve no preparation, and if feeling super adventurous can even go on toast (her main food group). See all recipes in this chapter for Clare's opinion.

What do you love about living in a share house and what are some of the challenges?

Some of the things we love:

Always having company, someone is always home to get packages, friends popping round to see someone else but you get to hang with them too, housemate dinners on the deck, more books to choose from, more clothes to steal. Most of all is probably the endless debriefs and chance to chat and share your life with people who become family.

Some of the challenges:

Comedic quantities of recycling, keeping a big house clean when everyone's on different schedules, and the endless socks and undies that no one claims, but remain, eternally around the washing machine.

What gives you and your housemates hope for a better world?

As we write this, half of Brisbane is under water in the second 'once in 100 year' flood since we all finished high school, and war has just broken out in Ukraine. There are a lot of reasons to despair. We take some solace in our home and community, where we share both grief and hope. It all feels a bit lighter and easier to process when it's shared. We all find hope in other places too – in the soil, on the streets, in the trees and the ocean, and in art. ✽

Banana bundt with date swirl & brown sugar glaze

Serves 10–12 · Vegan · Gluten Free

100 g (½ cup) dates, pitted and chopped

½ tsp bicarbonate of soda (baking soda)

250 ml (1 cup) boiling water

3 bananas (about 250 g/9 oz), mashed

185 ml (¾ cup) vegetable oil (or another neutral oil)

185 ml (¾ cup) milk of your choice

1½ tbsp tahini

40 g (2 tbsp) honey or maple syrup

125 g (⅔ cup) brown sugar

½ tsp ground cinnamon

450 g (3 cups) self-raising flour (or use gluten-free self-raising flour)

½ tsp salt

edible dried flowers, to decorate (optional)

Icing

75 g (2¾ oz) margarine or butter of your choice

125 g (⅔ cup) brown sugar

1 tsp vanilla essence

40 g (⅓ cup) icing (confectioners') sugar, plus extra if needed

This is a delicious, easy cake that makes a perfect morning or afternoon tea. It's vegan, not too sweet, and you probably already have all of the ingredients in your pantry. The date swirl and brown sugar glaze give the cake a lovely hit of caramel-ish sweetness, reminiscent of sticky date pudding. If you don't have a bundt tin, just make the cake in a regular cake or loaf tin. Take care to grease the tin well and give it a good bang on your kitchen bench or the floor once the cake is cooked to prevent the cake sticking.

Preheat the oven to 160°C (320°F) fan-forced. Thoroughly grease a bundt tin.

Combine the chopped dates, bicarbonate of soda and boiling water in a small saucepan and bring to a simmer over medium heat. Cook for a few minutes, until the dates have softened and formed a thick, chunky paste. Remove from the heat and set aside to cool a little.

Place the banana, vegetable oil, milk, tahini, honey or maple syrup, brown sugar and cinnamon in a mixing bowl and whisk until combined. Add the flour and salt and use a spoon or a spatula to gently fold the flour through. Don't worry about getting it completely even, just fold until most of the flour is incorporated. Pour in the date mixture and turn it through the batter gently, without mixing it in completely so that it cooks through the cake in a separated swirl.

Pour the mixture into the prepared tin, then transfer to the oven and bake for 35–45 minutes, until a skewer inserted into the cake comes out clean. Remove it from the oven and allow to cool for 10 minutes, then firmly bang the tin on your kitchen bench or floor a couple of times to help release the cake from the tin. Place a wire rack on top and flip the cake to remove it from the tin. If it needs some help to come out, knock the bottom of the tin with a heavy spoon a few times. Leave the cake to cool on the wire rack until it's only slightly warm to touch.

Meanwhile, prepare the icing by melting the margarine or butter and brown sugar in a bowl in a microwave on High or in a small saucepan over low heat. Whisk to combine, then add the vanilla and icing sugar and whisk to form a glossy glaze, adding extra icing sugar or a little warm water, if needed, to achieve a thick, spoonable consistency. Once the cake is mostly cooled, drizzle the glaze over the top, letting it slip down the sides, and decorate with edible dried flowers, if you like. ✳

Banoffee pavlova

Serves 10–12 · Gluten Free

100 g (3½ oz) dark chocolate (at least 70% cocoa solids)

6 egg whites (save the yolks for pasta dough, custard or carbonara)

230 g (1 cup) caster (superfine) sugar

2 tsp cornflour (corn starch)

2 tsp lemon juice or white vinegar

Dulce de leche

750 ml (3 cups) milk

125 g (⅔ cup) brown sugar

½ tsp bicarbonate of soda (baking soda)

pinch of flaky sea salt

Topping

400 ml (13½ fl oz) double-thickened (dollop) cream

4–5 bananas, thinly sliced on the diagonal

60 g (½ cup) toasted almonds, roughly chopped

½ tsp flaky sea salt

Swaps

Almonds – salted peanuts or crushed butter biscuits

The mother of all desserts, this is a showstopper that's sure to impress. With chocolate meringue and dulce de leche both made from scratch, this pav perhaps takes a little more effort than many of us have time for. Feel free to substitute a tin of dulce de leche, although I find the intensive act of waiting for milk and sugar to transform into a heavenly caramel incredibly satisfying and therapeutic. Plus it's less tooth-achingly sweet than tinned versions and will give you enough dulce de leche to use in milkshakes or atop a brownie batch later on.

Preheat the oven to 140°C (285°F) fan-forced and line a baking tray with baking paper.

Set a heatproof bowl over a saucepan of simmering water, add the chocolate and stir until melted. Set aside to cool slightly. This can also be done in a microwave on High, in 20–30 second bursts, stirring well in between.

In a clean, dry bowl, beat the egg whites with electric beaters until soft peaks form, then, working slowly, add the sugar 1 tablespoon at a time, beating well after each addition. It's tempting to rush this process, but be patient or your pavlova will weep when cooked. Keep whisking until the meringue is stiff and shiny and all the sugar is incorporated. Finally, add the cornflour and lemon juice or vinegar and whisk well to combine. Gently spoon the chocolate into the bowl and use a spatula to swirl it just once through the meringue. The chocolate will incorporate further as you scoop the meringue onto the tray and it's important to not mix it too thoroughly, both because the fat content will prevent the meringue from cooking, and because the ripple of chocolate looks incredible once cooked and cooled.

Carefully spoon the meringue onto the baking paper to form a large circle that's about 5 cm (2 in) high. Transfer to the oven and bake for about 2 hours, checking after 1 hour or so to ensure that the top isn't beginning to brown. If it is, reduce the temperature to 120°C (250°F). Once the meringue is firm to touch on the outside, turn the oven off and leave the meringue inside to cool completely. This will take about 2 hours, but you can also leave the meringue overnight. Store the meringue in an airtight container or wrapped up to keep it crisp until you're ready to serve.

Meanwhile, prepare the dulce de leche. Combine the milk and sugar in a saucepan over medium heat, whisking often until the sugar dissolves. Continue to heat the milk for 5 minutes or until hot, then add the bicarb soda, reduce the heat to very low and cook, stirring frequently, for 45–60 minutes, until the milk mixture becomes silky and thickens to a 'milk jam' (dulce de leche). Add the salt, then remove from the heat and set aside to cool completely.

To assemble the pavlova, top the meringue with the cream, swirling it around to cover most of the base. Spoon over about half the dulce de leche (save the rest in your fridge – it will keep for a week or two), then top with the banana and almonds and finish with the sea salt. Serve immediately. Any leftovers will keep in an airtight container in the fridge for 1–2 days. ✳

Miso & banana cream pie

Serves 8–10

125 g (1¼ cups) rye flour, plus extra if needed and for dusting

55 g (½ cup) almond meal (or other crushed nuts)

½ tsp salt

2 tbsp caster (superfine) sugar

50 g (1¾ oz) cold salted butter, roughly chopped

about 80 ml (⅓ cup) ice-cold water

whipped cream or vanilla ice cream, to serve

Banana custard filling

2 bananas

3 eggs

145 g (⅔ cup) caster (superfine) sugar

150 ml (5 fl oz) thickened (double/heavy) cream

1 tsp vanilla essence

250 g (9 oz) cream cheese

1 heaped tbsp miso paste

Swaps

Miso – 2 tbsp peanut butter plus 2 tsp soy sauce or tamari

Rye flour – wholemeal (whole-wheat) or plain (all-purpose) flour (reduce the water quantity to 70 ml/2 ¼ fl oz)

It might sound strange, but if you haven't yet discovered the joys of miso in sweet dishes, I implore you to give it a try. The umami saltiness of the miso adds a caramel flavour to this pie that is super delicious with the banana, and complements the nutty, solid crust well. It's the kind of pie I imagine you might find in an American diner – and really must be served with whipped cream on the side. It does require a little forward planning as the pie should be served cold, though you could pop it into the freezer to speed things up. You can use regular almond or another nut meal, but I usually just blitz up whatever nuts I have on hand in a food processor into a rough crumb, as it's nice to keep a bit of texture in the crust.

Combine the rye flour, almond meal, salt and sugar in a bowl. Add the chopped butter and use your fingers to rub it into the dry ingredients, until it is roughly dispersed throughout – this will take a few minutes. Don't worry if there are some visible bits of butter remaining. Pour in most of the water and use a fork to mix it through the buttered mixture, then use your hands to bring the mixture into a rough dough, adding the remaining water if needed and working to incorporate any dry bits of dough (if the dough is too sticky, dust your hands or the dough with a little more rye flour). Place the ball of dough in a bowl and cover, or wrap up well. Transfer to the fridge for about 30 minutes, to allow the butter to solidify again.

Preheat the oven to 180°C (350°F) fan-forced.

Dust your work surface with a little flour, then roll the dough into a 30 cm (12 in) circle, patching any tears as you go and taking care to keep the circle as even as possible. Roll the pastry gently onto the rolling pin, then transfer it to a 28 cm (11 in) pie tin, ideally one with a removable base. Due to the nut meal, this pastry is very tear-prone so don't stress if it breaks as you transfer it. Just use your fingers to repair any damage, while also pressing the pastry into the edge and side of the tin to create a tart shell. Prick the base a few times with a fork, then cover the pastry with a piece of baking paper and add 1–2 cups of dried beans, rice or baking beads. Transfer to the oven and cook for 10 minutes, then remove the beans and baking paper and cook for a further 5 minutes. Remove from the oven and set aside.

To create the banana custard filling, blitz the ingredients in a food processor. Alternatively, mash the bananas in a bowl until completely smooth, add the remaining ingredients and whisk until smooth. The mixture should look very liquidy. Pour the banana custard into the pie shell, then carefully transfer the pie to the oven, reduce the temperature to 160°C (320°F) and cook for 30–40 minutes, until the filling is set and the crust is golden. If it looks like the crust is burning, cover with foil and continue to cook until the filling is set.

Remove the pie from the oven and allow it to cool a little, then transfer to the fridge to cool completely before serving alongside some whipped cream or vanilla ice cream. ✳

Fudgy double chocolate cookies

Makes 15–20 · Vegan

1 small banana (or ½ large)

170 ml (⅔ cup) vegetable oil
(or another neutral oil)

1 tbsp tahini

185 g (1 cup) brown sugar

2 tsp vanilla essence

1 tsp flaky sea salt

40 g (⅓ cup) Dutch-processed
cocoa powder

185 g (1¼ cups) plain (all-purpose)
flour

1 tsp bicarbonate of soda
(baking soda)

150 g (5½ oz) mixed vegan chocolate
chips or chunks

Cookies are one of the things I tend to largely steer clear of veganising. I find that without eggs and butter, either their texture sucks or they end up tasting distinctly of vegan margarine in a way I really don't love. But these cookies! I am obsessed. They're not even just yum 'for a vegan cookie', I think they're actually just yum. The banana acts as a binder, assisting with a chewy, brownie-like texture and some extra sweetness. Unlike in many banana-baked goods, I prefer not to use overripe bananas, as they add too strong a flavour. Also, chocolate is the real hero here, so use good cocoa powder, and ideally a mix of types of chocolate chips (I like some super dark and some more milky).

Blend or mash the banana until smooth. Add the vegetable oil, tahini, sugar and vanilla and whisk well until smooth.

In a separate bowl, whisk together the salt, cocoa powder, flour and bicarbonate of soda (sift the bicarb soda if it looks clumpy). Add the dry ingredients to the wet ingredients and use a wooden spoon to mix gently until just combined. Add the chocolate chips and stir through to combine. Transfer to the fridge for at least 30 minutes or the freezer for 15 minutes to firm up (the uncooked dough will also keep for up to 2 days in the fridge).

Preheat the oven to 180°C (350°F) fan-forced and line a large baking tray with baking paper.

Roll the cookie dough into 15–20 evenly sized balls and place them on the baking tray, pressing them slightly to flatten and leaving space between each one to allow for spreading.

Bake the cookies for 12–15 minutes, until they're just cracked and have spread into a nice cookie shape. Remove from the oven and leave to cool. They'll harden and shrink a little, but don't worry if they feel very soft.

Enjoy the cookies warm and fresh, or leave them to cool completely in the fridge. Store any leftovers in an airtight container in the fridge for a few days, or in the freezer for up to 2 months. *

Mini banana & gingernut tiramisus

Makes 8

6 egg yolks (freeze the whites to use the next time you make meringue, see my pavlova recipe on page 47)

2 tsp vanilla essence

75 g (⅓ cup) caster (superfine) sugar

½ tsp salt

300 ml (10 fl oz) double-thickened (dollop) cream

300 g (10½ oz) mascarpone, at room temperature

4 shots of espresso (or 125 ml/½ cup very strong black coffee)

125 ml (½ cup) amaro or other liqueur or fortified wine of choice

200 g (7 oz) gingernut biscuits (cookies)

2–3 bananas, thinly sliced

50 g (1¾ oz) dark chocolate

Swaps

Gingernut biscuits – savoiardi biscuits, or another biscuit of choice

Mascarpone – 2:1 mix of softened cream cheese and extra double-thickened cream

These individual tiramisus are such a special way to finish a meal with friends or family. The very untraditional additions of banana and gingernut biscuits in place of Italian sponge fingers lend the dessert a whole new flavour profile that I adore. My favourite alcohol to use is amaro – an Italian herb liqueur that's sweet, but with a very earthy flavour. Substitute any alcohol you have on hand that has a little sweetness – brandy, port, coffee liqueur all work very well, or leave it out altogether, if you prefer. Although a little fiddly to prepare, these tiramisus can (and should ideally) be made a full day ahead.

Set a heatproof bowl over a saucepan of gently simmering water, then add the egg yolks, vanilla, sugar and salt. If you don't have a bowl and saucepan that fit the bill, you can put the ingredients directly in a saucepan, but cook over the lowest heat possible. Whisk the egg-yolk mixture until it begins to gently warm, then continue whisking for a few minutes, until the mixture turns pale, thick and creamy, like custard. Remove the bowl from the saucepan and set aside to cool.

Meanwhile, whisk the cream and mascarpone together by hand, or using electric beaters on low speed, until combined. Pour in the cooled egg-yolk mixture and keep whisking until you have stiff peaks.

Stir the espresso and alcohol together in a small bowl.

Assemble the tiramisus in small glasses or bowls (you can also use one larger dish). Scoop a dessert spoon of the whipped cream into each glass or bowl. Dunk a gingernut biscuit in the coffee mixture, submerging it for a couple of seconds, then place the soaked biscuit on top of the cream. Top with another spoonful of cream, then add a few slices of banana and another coffee-dunked biscuit. Finish with a few more pieces of banana and a final spoonful of cream (distributing it evenly among the glasses or bowls). Transfer to the fridge and leave to set for at least 6 hours, or overnight.

Right before serving, finely grate the chocolate over each tiramisu. ✳

Broccoli

Recipes

Broccoli is one of those magical vegetables that shines both completely raw and almost-too-charred and, of course, everywhere in between. It's packed with good nutritious stuff, and it holds its own when cooked, making it a good vessel for flavour and sauces. It's a veg I only really got into cooking in a big way in the last few years, but now I find it oddly addictive, and use it at just about every chance possible. These recipes are a broad selection of some of my favourite broccoli dishes, but you could also swap in broccoli in heaps of the recipes in this book, so buy in bulk whenever it's in season. Oh, and do make sure to use the whole broccoli every time! Using both the florets and stalks means lots of interesting texture and no waste.

With Tammy, Will, Ben, Allisa and Jacquie

Describe your household

We are a culturally diverse LGBTQI+ household that really does operate as a family. We are five big and vibrant personalities that all somehow complement each other. There's Will who is studying to become a nurse and currently working as a dental assistant, Tam is studying psychology and working as a support worker, Jacquie works in law and is preparing for a trip to Spain, Ben is a cognitive neuroscience PhD candidate and Allisa is a lawyer by day, but is involved in a bunch of creative and philanthropic projects on the side. We all have very busy lives, but we manage to come together for support and community. We have all become incredibly close and share many activities, even outside of the house, too. We have created a home and it's always so comforting to walk through the door after a long day and debrief with each other.

Do you share food as a household? How often and what does that involve?

We share our basics: garlic, onions, condiments, sauces and rice. In our house we have a mix of Japanese, Peruvian, Thai and Australian cooking. We try to limit food waste as much as possible by sharing certain ingredients. We will often come together for a big, shared meal when our schedules line up. This has happened a lot more during the various lockdowns. Even when we cook separately, we tend to eat our individual meals together at the table with whoever is home. This results in us sharing bits of those meals and trying each other's dishes, which is also helpful in limiting food waste!

What's your favourite way to cook/eat broccoli?

This is a hard one! I think the general consensus is either in a stir-fry with oyster sauce or as a side dish, with parmesan, panko, toasted almonds and lemon.

What do you love about living in a share house generally, or about this house in particular?

Share-house living creates a sense of family and community. It's a unique relationship where you can benefit from the support and warmth of a friendship or family, but also have the respect and consciousness of a contributing house member or partnership. We absolutely love coming together after a long day at work, sharing the stories from the day and having a vent. All congregating around the living and dining room while we take turns to cook, sharing dating stories, playing music and getting too excited for one another. We are each other's hype people, counsel and, at times, only voice of reason. *

Satay broccoli mince with soba noodles

Serves 4–6 · Vegan · Gluten Free

60 ml (¼ cup) vegetable oil (or another neutral oil)

6–7 spring onions (scallions), finely chopped

200 g (7 oz) firm tofu, crumbled

4 garlic cloves, finely chopped

small bunch of coriander (cilantro), stems washed and finely chopped, leaves picked

400 g (14 oz) broccoli (about 1 large head), stalks and florets finely chopped to resemble coarse breadcrumbs

2 tbsp lime juice

450 g (1 lb) soba noodles (use rice noodles for gluten free)

Coconut–peanut sauce

40 g (1½ oz) ginger, peeled and finely grated

125 ml (½ cup) soy sauce or tamari

60 ml (¼ cup) rice wine vinegar

2 tbsp peanut butter

1 tbsp tahini

250 ml (1 cup) coconut cream

salt and pepper

To serve

toasted sesame seeds

thinly sliced long red chilli

lime wedges

Swaps

Broccoli – lentils, cauliflower, mushroom or cabbage and some shredded stir-fry greens

Though it won't win any awards for its looks, this makes for an incredibly satisfying dinner that feels like comfort food, even though it's full of healthy ingredients. Crumbled tofu and finely chopped or blitzed broccoli pieces are cooked down to create a mince-like texture, and drowned in a deliciously fragrant peanut sauce that clings to the soba noodles when you toss it through. Sesame seeds and fresh herbs scattered over the top brighten things up, and you could serve this with a swirl of vegan Kewpie mayonnaise and chilli sauce.

To make the coconut–peanut sauce, whisk the ginger, soy sauce, rice wine vinegar, peanut butter, tahini, coconut cream and a pinch of salt and pepper in a bowl and set aside.

Heat the vegetable oil in a large frying pan over high heat. Add the spring onion, reserving a handful or so to scatter over the final dish, and cook for 1 minute, then add the tofu and cook, stirring frequently, for 5 or so minutes, until the tofu starts to brown and stick a little to the base of the pan. Stir through the garlic and cook for 1–2 minutes, then add the coriander stems and broccoli and toss or stir to mix well. Cook for 3–4 minutes, until the broccoli has cooked down a little, then pour in the satay sauce and toss or stir well to combine. Add 125 ml (½ cup) of water, then reduce the heat to low and simmer for 3–4 minutes, until the sauce has thickened a little. Remove the pan from the heat until ready to serve, to retain some crunch in the broccoli.

Meanwhile, bring a large saucepan of water to the boil and add the soba noodles. Cook for 1 minute less than the packet directions to ensure that they don't overcook and become gluggy. Drain in a colander and run under cold water for 30 seconds – this is a really important step, as it removes any excess starch from the noodles and prevents them from sticking together. Transfer to a serving bowl.

Stir the lime juice through the broccoli and tofu mixture, then spoon the mixture over the soba noodles. I like to serve this with all of the mixture on top and stir it through as I'm eating it, but you could also toss to combine before serving. Scatter over the toasted sesame seeds, red chilli and coriander leaves, and serve warm with lime wedges on the side. ✳

Broccoli & cheddar croquettes with ranch dipping sauce

Serves 4–6 or 10–12 as a snack

700 g (1 lb 9 oz) potatoes (yukon golds, dutch creams or russets all work especially well here), peeled and quartered

salt and pepper

400 g (14 oz) broccoli (about 1 large head), stems and florets roughly chopped

50 g (1¾ oz) salted butter, melted

2 tbsp white miso paste

3–4 spring onions (scallions), finely chopped

zest of 1 lemon

100 g (1 cup) grated sharp cheddar

2 egg yolks

75 g (½ cup) plain (all-purpose) flour

Crumb coating

2 eggs

125 ml (½ cup) milk

150 g (1 cup) plain (all-purpose) flour

1 tsp salt

1 heaped tsp smoky paprika

120–180 g (2–3 cups) panko or homemade breadcrumbs

1–2 litres (34–68 fl oz) vegetable oil (or another neutral oil)

These croquettes are delightfully creamy, but pack in a good whack of broccoli too, giving them a nice freshness that counteracts the rich flavour. Miso is the secret ingredient, providing a delicious savouriness and depth that complements the sharp cheddar. I've fried my croquettes but you could absolutely bake them to make them healthier. They'll lose a bit of their shape cooked this way, but with a bit of oil sprayed or drizzled over the top they'll still crisp up nicely.

Place the potato in a large saucepan and cover with cold water. Add a heavy dash of salt, place the pan over medium heat and bring to a slow simmer. Cook for 20 minutes or until the potato is soft and a knife easily passes through without resistance. Using tongs, transfer the potato to a large bowl.

Add the broccoli to the same hot, salty water and blanch for 2 minutes or until bright green and slightly softened. Drain the broccoli and leave to cool for a few minutes before finely chopping or blitzing in a food processor, until it forms a chunky crumb that is consistent in size.

Add the melted butter and miso paste to the bowl with the potato and use a potato masher or ricer to gently crush the soft potato to form a creamy mash consistency. Be careful not to overmix and turn the potato into glue. Add the broccoli, spring onion, lemon zest, cheddar, egg yolks and flour to the bowl and stir a few times to combine the ingredients. Taste and season with salt and pepper, then set the mixture aside in the fridge for about 30 minutes to firm up.

Set up your crumbing station by whisking the eggs and milk together in one bowl, combining the flour, salt and paprika in another and placing the breadcrumbs in a final large, shallow bowl.

If you're frying the croquettes, pour 3–4 cm (1½–1¾ in) of oil into a large saucepan and heat over medium heat. If baking the croquettes, line a large baking tray with baking paper and preheat the oven to 200°C (400°F) fan-forced.

Form golf ball–sized portions of the croquette mixture into small egg shapes, then toss each croquette in the flour mixture, shaking off any excess. Next, dunk the croquettes into the egg wash and finish by rolling them in the breadcrumbs, pressing the crumbs onto the croquettes to help them stick. Once the oil is hot enough (test by dropping in a few breadcrumbs – if they sizzle, then the oil is ready), fry the croquettes in batches, ensuring that they don't touch each other and gently turning once or twice as they cook, for 3–4 minutes, until deep golden brown and crunchy. If you're baking the croquettes, spread them evenly across the prepared tray and drizzle with some oil. Bake for 30 or so minutes, turning halfway through cooking, until the croquettes are crunchy and golden.

Prepare the ranch sauce by whisking all the ingredients together in a small bowl. Serve the croquettes warm alongside the sauce. *

Ranch dipping sauce

125 g (½ cup) natural yoghurt

90 g (⅓ cup) Kewpie mayonnaise

1 tbsp apple cider vinegar

2 tbsp dill fronds, finely chopped
(or 2 tsp dried)

½ tsp smoky paprika

1 tsp mustard powder

½ tsp salt

Swaps

*Gluten free – plain flour: rice flour or
gluten-free plain flour; breadcrumbs:
polenta or gluten-free breadcrumbs*

*Vegan – butter: vegan margarine; egg
yolks: 1 chia/flax egg; milk and egg
wash: 250 ml (1 cup) plant-based milk;
ranch dipping sauce: vegan yoghurt
and mayo*

Roasted broccoli green curry & coconut rice

Serves 4–6 · Vegan · Gluten Free

500 g (1 lb 2 oz) broccoli (about 2 small heads), stalks and florets roughly chopped or torn

60 ml (¼ cup) vegetable oil (or another neutral oil), plus extra if needed

salt and pepper

400 ml (14 fl oz) tin coconut milk

2 tbsp soy sauce or tamari

Green curry paste

1 long green chilli (deseeded if you prefer less spice)

40 g (1 heaped cup) coriander (cilantro) stems and leaves

5–6 spring onions (scallions), roughly chopped

1 tbsp brown sugar

40–50 g (1½–1¾ oz) ginger, peeled and roughly chopped

5 garlic cloves, peeled

1 tsp ground cumin

1 tbsp lime juice

2 lemongrass stalks, white part only, roughly chopped (or 1 tbsp crushed lemongrass)

2 tbsp vegan fish sauce

4–5 makrut lime leaves (or 1 tsp jarred shredded leaves)

50 g (1 packed cup) leafy greens, such as spinach, bok choy, kale, choy sum, gai lan or mustard greens

salt and pepper

The trick to this super-vibrant green curry is to add a bunch of blitzed leafy greens into the paste which gives it such a lovely, bright-green colour. I like serving this simply with charred broccoli pieces, enabling them to be the star of the show, but of course you could throw in more vegetables or some tofu. The lime leaves and lemongrass are really essential for the beautiful flavour of the paste, so if you can't find fresh, spring for jars of the preserved stuff, which will keep in your fridge for ages for future use. Serve the curry alongside some roti or with this delicious coconut rice.

Preheat the oven to 220°C (430°F) fan-forced. Scatter the broccoli in a large baking dish, drizzle over half the vegetable oil and season with salt and pepper. Roast for 15–20 minutes, turning once halfway through cooking.

Meanwhile, for the coconut rice, rinse the rice well, then place in a saucepan with the coconut cream, salt and 625 ml (2½ cups) of water. Bring to the boil over medium heat and cook, stirring once after 5 minutes of cooking, for 15 minutes or until the rice is tender. Remove from the heat, cover with a lid and set aside until ready to serve.

To make the green curry paste, blitz the ingredients in a high-powered blender or food processor to form a smooth, green curry paste, adding a little water if necessary to get the mixture moving. Taste and adjust the seasoning and spice as required.

Heat the remaining oil in a frying pan over medium heat. Add the green curry paste and cook, stirring frequently, for 3–4 minutes, until the paste is fragrant and bubbling. Add the coconut milk and stir well to combine. Bring the curry to a slow simmer and cook for 2 minutes. Taste and adjust the seasoning as needed.

Drizzle the soy sauce over the charred broccoli and toss to combine, then add the broccoli to the curry sauce, stirring it through if you like, or leaving it on top.

Fluff the rice with a fork, then transfer to a serving bowl and top with the crispy fried shallot. Serve with the green curry, straight from the pan. *

Coconut rice

400 g (2 cups) jasmine or
long-grain rice

200 ml (7 fl oz) coconut cream

½ tsp salt

2 tbsp crispy fried shallots, to serve

Swaps

*Broccoli – snow peas, zucchini,
broccolini, gai lan*

Shaved broccoli & avocado salad

Serves 6–8 as a side · Vegan · Gluten Free

100 g (⅔ cup) almonds, roughly chopped

1 tbsp soy sauce or tamari

600 g (1 lb 5 oz) broccoli (about 2 small–medium heads), stalks and florets finely chopped or sliced

½ red onion, finely diced

1½ avocados, chopped into 1 cm (½ in) cubes

20 g (1 cup) flat-leaf parsley, chopped

<u>Chickpea dressing</u>

400 g (14 oz) tin chickpeas (garbanzo beans), including the soaking liquid

1 tbsp tahini

½ avocado

1 tbsp maple syrup

1 tbsp lime juice, plus extra if needed

30 g (1 cup) coriander (cilantro) leaves

2 tbsp soy sauce or tamari

salt and pepper

Please. Make. This. Salad. It's so easy and quick to make (especially if you use a mandoline or food processor to chop all the broccoli), as well as being delicious and moreish, and a perfect way to eat a big bowl of raw vegetables when that urge strikes. The dressing really carries the salad – it's super hearty and coats everything generously in a soft green blanket. The smoky, salty nuts finish it off beautifully with some welcome crunch. You could add some extra veggies or sub out some of the broccoli for peas or broad beans, and serve with some falafels or veggie patties for a delicious dinner.

Heat a frying pan over medium heat and add the almonds. Cook, stirring often, for a few minutes, until they begin to brown. Turn off the heat, drizzle over the soy sauce and stir to combine – the soy sauce will sizzle and evaporate quickly. Remove the almonds from the pan and set aside to cool.

Prepare the chickpea dressing by blending all of the ingredients in a blender or food processor to a thick, smoothie-like consistency. Taste and add additional seasoning or lime juice if needed. The dressing is mild in flavour, but it's important that it has a hum of seasoning and citrus.

Combine all the remaining salad ingredients in a large bowl, mixing them well to combine. Pour the dressing over the top and toss to coat the veggies. Transfer to a serving dish, or wipe down the edge of the bowl you're using. Scatter over the toasted almonds and serve. ✳

Charred broccoli carbonara

Serves 4–6 · Gluten Free

salt and pepper

2 heads of broccoli, sliced into
4–6 slabs each, stalks included

60 ml (¼ cup) olive oil

5 garlic cloves, thinly sliced

500 g (1 lb 2 oz) pasta of your choice

4 egg yolks (freeze the egg whites
to use in other recipes)

2 whole eggs

100 g (1 cup) grated parmesan,
plus extra to serve

2 tsp chopped thyme leaves
(or 1 tsp dried)

3 heaped tbsp crispy fried onions

dill fronds, to serve

Swaps

*Broccoli – broccolini, asparagus, gai
lan, mushrooms or kale*

*Crispy fried onions – toasted fresh
breadcrumbs*

Crispy fried onions, which you'll find in any Asian grocery store, or near the curry pastes in the supermarket, are the hero here. They add a satisfying crunch and savouriness to the pasta which, when combined with the smoky barbecued broccoli and hefty portion of pepper and parmesan, creates a flavour reminiscent of pancetta in a traditional carbonara. This is a quick meal, easy to throw together in the time it takes to cook the pasta, and manages to incorporate a surprising amount of broccoli. Broccolini would also be perfect, as would zucchini, mushrooms or green beans when broccoli isn't in season. If you don't have a barbecue, you can cook the broccoli in batches in a frying pan over high heat to get some of that smoky flavour.

Preheat a barbecue flat plate or heavy-based frying pan until it's smoking hot. As it heats, fill your largest saucepan with water, add 1–2 tablespoons of salt and bring to the boil.

Drizzle the broccoli with the olive oil and season with salt and pepper. Place the broccoli on the barbecue flat plate and close the lid (if it has one), or add to the frying pan, and cook for 5–7 minutes, until some of the edges are charred. Flip the broccoli over, scatter with the garlic and close the lid again for another 5 or so minutes, letting the garlic cook gently in the steam and indirect heat from the broccoli. Once the broccoli is cooked through and nicely charred on both sides, transfer to a chopping board and let it cool for a few minutes before chopping it into small (less than 1 cm/½ in) chunks.

Meanwhile, add the pasta to the boiling water and cook, stirring occasionally, for 2 minutes less than the packet instructions.

While the pasta cooks, combine the egg yolks, whole eggs, parmesan, 1–2 teaspoons of freshly ground black pepper and the thyme in a bowl.

Scoop out a mugful of the pasta cooking water and set aside. Drain the pasta and return it to the pan over low heat. Add the broccoli and half the pasta water, tossing well to combine, then cook for a couple of minutes, until the water has disappeared and the mixture is steaming hot.

Remove the pan from the heat. Add the remaining pasta water to the egg mixture, stirring well to combine, then slowly drizzle the mixture into the pasta, mixing as you go until the pasta is evenly coated.

Serve immediately, scattered with extra parmesan, a generous sprinkling of the crispy fried onions and a few dill fronds. ✽

Capsicum

Recipes

When cooked or prepared poorly, capsicums (bell peppers) are one of my least favourite vegetables – I find them dominant and bitter. But when the right variety and colour is chosen for the job, and it's cooked and paired well, the capsicum can be an absolute hero. Charred until soft and silky inside, or roasted and blended into sauces, like the romesco sauce in this chapter, capsicums are transformed. I've suggested which colour capsicums to use in these recipes, and I've only used the most easily accessible bell variety, though you could substitute other colours or members of the capsicum family in these dishes.

With Maddie and Liv

Describe your household

We met at architecture school while doing our master's. We have similar lifestyles and friends, so living together is easy.

Do you share food as a household? How often and what does that involve?

We share all our food. Everything is a free for all. We go to the shops together and buy our own groceries. We usually do our own thing for lunch, but we share the food we cook and cook dinner together maybe three times a week.

What's your favourite way to cook/eat capsicums?

Our favourite dish that wouldn't be the same without capsicum is patatas a lo pobre (poor man's potatoes). It's a one-pan wonder and capsicum is the star of the show. You only need these ingredients:

2 onions, chopped

4 garlic cloves, chopped

2 capsicums, chopped

2–3 large potatoes, thinly sliced

Put everything into a pan with lots and lots of olive oil and salt, and cook over medium heat for about 45 minutes, until the potato is cooked through and everything is slightly caramelised. It's best served straight from the pan at the table.

What does a typical Saturday morning in your house look like?

We usually get a coffee from our local cafe Vvaldmeer and sit on the balcony in the sun. We love doing the *Good Weekend* quiz, but never get more than 11 points, so we've recently started quiz training during the week in the hope that we can consistently score 13 or more. Saturdays are usually pretty lazy because Friday nights are not ...

What do you love about living in a share house generally, or about this house in particular?

Our apartment feels like a hot-air balloon with lots of light and views to the trees and city. The experience of the space changes dramatically from morning to night and in different weather. Our balcony, although small, is the perfect place to wind down or watch a storm. When it's bad weather we love to recline inside with a wine. ✳

Silky capsicums with ricotta cream & radishes

Serves 8–10 as a snack or starter · Gluten Free

6–7 large mixed capsicums (bell peppers) or long Italian peppers (cubanelles)

60 ml (¼ cup) olive oil, plus extra for drizzling

2 tsp red wine vinegar

flaky sea salt and pepper

300 g (10½ oz) smooth ricotta

100 ml (3½ oz) thickened (double/heavy) cream

zest of 1 small lemon (about 2 tsp)

4–5 radishes, thinly sliced (use a mandoline or food processor to do this)

handful of mint leaves

sourdough or focaccia bread, to serve

Swaps

Vegan – ricotta and cream: cashew cream, hummus or avocado blended with some plant-based milk

Ricotta – cream cheese or crème fraîche

The next time you see capsicums super cheap and in season, grab a stack and cook them this way, even if they aren't normally a go-to vegetable for you. Any colour will do, but I love using a mix. Blanching them, then cooking at a screaming-hot temperature ensures that they slip out of their skins easily, and develop a soft, smoky flavour that's far better than the slightly tinny taste of their jarred equivalents. The combination of flavours and textures in this dish are luscious and satisfying, particularly the crunch of super-thin radishes, showered over the top. This dish is great (if a little messy) at a picnic, or makes a classy starter, served in individual portions alongside some fresh sourdough to scoop it all onto.

Fill your largest saucepan with water and bring to the boil. Heat a barbecue flat plate or oven to its hottest temperature.

Lower the capsicums into the boiling water and cook for 2–3 minutes, then drain and set aside to cool a little. Transfer the capsicums to the barbecue, or to a baking tray and into the oven. Cook, turning every 10 minutes, for about 25 minutes on the barbecue or about 40 minutes in the oven, until they're charred and mostly blackened all over. Set aside until cool enough to handle, then slip off the skins and discard them, along with the stalks and seeds. Use your hands to tear the flesh into long, thin strips and place them in a bowl. Add the olive oil, vinegar and about a teaspoon each of flaky sea salt and cracked black pepper, and mix well.

Meanwhile, in a separate bowl, combine the ricotta, cream and lemon zest, along with a generous sprinkle of salt, then spread the mixture onto a large serving plate. Top with the capsicum, then scatter over the radish and mint leaves. Finish with an extra drizzle of olive oil and a sprinkle of salt. Serve alongside sourdough bread, to mop everything up. ✳

Eggs menemen with simit

Serves 4–6 (with a few simit to spare)

60 ml (¼ cup) olive oil

2 green capsicums (bell peppers), finely diced

1 large brown onion, finely diced

1 long green chilli, deseeded and finely diced (optional)

4 large tomatoes, finely diced

1 tsp dried thyme (or 1 tbsp fresh leaves)

salt and pepper

6 eggs

basil leaves, to serve

butter, to serve

Simit

310 ml (1¼ cups) warm water

½ tsp instant dried yeast

500 g (1 lb 2 oz) bread flour, plus extra if needed and for dusting

1 heaped tsp salt

Simit topping

3 tbsp golden syrup

60 ml (¼ cup) water

2 tbsp plain (all-purpose) flour

pinch of salt

100 g (⅔ cup) toasted sesame seeds

Swaps

Vegan – eggs: 400 g (14 oz) silken tofu

Bread flour – plain (all-purpose) flour

Golden syrup – honey or maple syrup

When travelling around Turkey for a couple of months, I ate both menemen and simit almost every day – sometimes alongside each other; other times not. Both rely on such simple processes and pantry staples, but will make delicious and interesting additions to your cooking repertoire. I love the way the capsicum transforms when cooked for so long in lashings of olive oil, to become sweet and jammy – it's sure to win over even the most sceptical green-capsicum haters. Because simit requires very little rising time, you can make these bagel-like sesame breads in just over an hour. Serve the simit and menemen together, or separately, for breakfast, lunch or dinner.

First, get the simit started by whisking the warm water and yeast together in a large bowl. Leave to stand for a few minutes, then stir in the flour and salt. Bring the mixture together with your hands to form a sticky dough, then keep kneading it in the bowl or on a lightly floured work surface for 3–5 minutes, until it becomes soft and pliable. You could do this in a stand mixer with a dough hook if you prefer. If the dough is sticking to your fingers, add an extra sprinkling of flour. When you've finished kneading, form the dough into a ball, return it to the bowl and cover with a tea towel. Leave the dough to rise for at least 30 minutes, while you start the menemen.

Heat the olive oil in a large cast-iron or non-stick frying pan over high heat. Add the capsicum and onion and cook, stirring frequently, for 10 or so minutes, until the vegetables are starting to brown. Add the chilli (if using) and tomato and cook for 5–10 minutes, stirring often. Reduce the heat to low and continue to cook for another 15–20 minutes, until everything has broken down to a soft, jammy paste. Stir through the thyme and a generous pinch each of salt and pepper, then turn off the heat and leave the mixture in the pan until you're almost ready to serve.

Preheat the oven to 220°C (430°F) fan-forced and line a baking tray with baking paper.

Whisk the simit topping ingredients, except the sesame seeds, and 60 ml (¼ cup) of water in a shallow bowl. Pour the sesame seeds into a second shallow bowl.

Tip the dough onto the work surface and cut it into eight even pieces. Leave the dough to relax for a few minutes. One by one, roll and stretch each piece of dough into a long, skinny rope about 30 cm (12 in) long. Working with one rope at a time, fold the rope in half, then work the two halves into a loosely twisted coil, folding them up and over each other. This can also be done by holding the folded rope of dough in the air and spinning it around itself. Connect the two ends to form a ring shape, then dunk the dough ring into the golden syrup mixture and then the sesame seeds, ensuring that the seeds thoroughly coat the top of the ring. Place on the tray and repeat with the remaining dough to make eight simit. →

Transfer the simit to the oven and bake for 20–25 minutes, until golden brown. Remove from the oven and transfer to a serving dish.

To finish the menemen, reheat the pan over medium heat. As the pan is warming up, crack in the eggs, then use a rubber spatula to break up the yolks and gently whisk the eggs to form a scramble, working them into the vegetable mixture. Once the mixture is warm and the egg is scrambled, taste a little and check the seasoning, adding salt and pepper if necessary.

Scatter a few basil leaves over the menemen and serve with the hot simit and some butter. ✳

Spicy capsicum & artichoke pesto with hand-rolled pasta

Serves 4–6 · Vegan

60 ml (¼ cup) olive oil, plus extra
for drizzling

250 g (9 oz) cherry tomatoes, halved

3 garlic cloves, sliced

500 g (1 lb 2 oz) roasted capsicum
(bell pepper) pieces

150 g (5½ oz) marinated artichoke
hearts, plus 60 ml (¼ cup) of soaking
oil or brine

80 g (½ cup) cashew nuts

2 tbsp capers, plus 1 tbsp of brine

30 g (1 cup) basil leaves, plus extra
to serve

1 x 400 g (14 oz) tin cannellini beans,
drained and rinsed

¼ tsp cayenne pepper

salt and pepper

Pici

500 g (1 lb 2 oz) 00 flour

1 tsp salt

2 tbsp olive oil

250 ml (1 cup) warm water

durum semolina or extra 00 flour,
for dusting

Although they don't beat homemade roasted capsicums (see page 80), jarred capsicums are incredibly cheap, versatile and usually pretty easy to find. This pesto-like sauce is deceptively creamy, despite being vegan, thanks to the blended artichokes and cannellini beans, and the little hint of spice makes it really moreish. I've served it here with some hand-rolled pasta, but the pesto is also delightful scooped on top of a bowl of roasted vegetables, as a base for crostini, or as a dip. The pici is very easy and makes a therapeutic (if a little time-consuming) afternoon activity, but feel free to substitute some packet pasta. The pesto will make more than you need for this dish, unless you like it super saucy, so keep the leftovers in the fridge for up to a week to use in other meals.

To make the pici, stir the flour and salt together in a large bowl until combined. Make a well in the centre and pour in the olive oil and warm water, then use a fork to bring the ingredients together into a rough ball. Knead the dough for 5–10 minutes, until soft and stretchy. Cover the dough with an upturned bowl or wrap in plastic wrap and leave to rest for at least 1 hour.

Dust a work surface with durum semolina or a little extra flour and divide the dough into about 12 pieces. Roll each piece until it's 10–15 cm (4–6 in) long, then cut each rope into 1 cm (½ in) thick strips. Use your hands to roll each strip into a thick noodle shape. If you're finding the dough isn't stretching and rolling easily, leave it for a few minutes then return and continue. Dust the pici well with more semolina or flour to prevent it sticking.

Leave the pasta to rest and dry out while you make the pesto. Heat the oil in a large frying pan over high heat. Add the cherry tomatoes and cook for 10 minutes, tossing occasionally, letting them stick and blister a bit. Stir in the garlic, then turn off the heat and allow the garlic to cook in the residual heat for a couple of minutes.

Place the tomato and garlic and remaining ingredients in a blender or food processor and blend or blitz until well combined. Taste and season well with salt and pepper.

Fill your largest saucepan with water and add 1–2 tablespoons of salt. Bring to a rapid boil, then add the pici and cook for 3–4 minutes, until they're chewy and just cooked through. Drain, reserving 250 ml (1 cup) of the pasta cooking water. Return the pici and reserved pasta water to the pan and add about half the pesto. Gently toss the pasta to coat in the pesto and cooking water until just combined. Serve with an extra drizzle of olive oil and a few basil leaves scattered over the top.

Store any leftover pesto in an airtight container in the fridge for a week or so. ✳

One-tray rice & bean bake

Serves 4–6 · Gluten Free

300 g (1½ cups) long-grain or basmati rice

375 ml (1½ cups) vegetable stock

60 ml (¼ cup) olive oil

2 tomatoes, finely diced

2 yellow capsicums (bell peppers), finely diced

1 small brown onion, finely diced

4 garlic cloves, minced

1 heaped tsp ground cumin

1 heaped tsp ground coriander

1 heaped tsp smoky paprika

1 heaped tsp dried oregano

500 g (2 cups) tomato passata (puréed tomatoes)

salt and pepper

1 x 400 g (14 oz) tin refried beans

70 g (2½ oz) grated cheddar

sour cream and/or guacamole, to serve (optional)

Coriander salsa verde

60 g (2 cups) coriander (cilantro) stems and leaves

35 g (¼ cup) pickled jalapenos, plus 60 ml (¼ cup) of the pickling liquid

1 tsp sugar

½ tsp salt

60 ml (¼ cup) olive oil

1 garlic clove

This meal is weeknight friendly, hands-off, easily veganised and feels far tastier than it should be, given its simplicity. It makes a great meal to drop on someone's doorstep, and will be delicious for a few days, kept in the fridge. Finely diced yellow capsicums are nestled in the rice, providing a sweetness and nice texture, but the real hero of this dish is definitely the refried beans which are up there with my favourite ingredients you can buy in a tin. I use premade beans mostly because part of the beauty of this meal is its speed, but you can easily make your own if you prefer (see note below). I've included a very easy coriander salsa, but you can also serve the bake with your preferred hot sauce.

Preheat the oven to 180°C (350°F) fan-forced.

Rinse the rice well under running water, then transfer to a large baking dish, similar to what you'd cook a lasagne in. Stir in the stock, olive oil, tomato, capsicum, onion, garlic, spices and dried oregano. Add about 375 g (1½ cups) of the passata and a generous pinch of salt and pepper, then gently stir to combine, ensuring that the veggies and spices are well distributed. Taste the liquid to make sure you've added enough seasoning – it should taste quite salty.

Combine the refried beans with the remaining passata and 125 ml (½ cup) of water. Spoon the bean mixture over the uncooked rice mix and spread it out in an even layer, leaving a 1–2 cm (½–¾ in) border around the edges.

Sprinkle over the cheese, then transfer to the oven and bake for 30–40 minutes, until the cheese is golden and the rice mix is bubbling up around the sides. Test a grain of rice to ensure that it's cooked through.

Meanwhile, to make the coriander salsa verde, combine all of the ingredients in a blender and blend on high speed until smooth, adding a splash of water, if necessary, to get the ingredients going. Taste the salsa and adjust the seasoning to taste. The salsa can be stored in the fridge for a week or two, and is brilliant on just about everything.

Serve the bake warm, alongside sour cream and/or guacamole, with the salsa verde drizzled over the top. ✳

Note: To make your own refried beans, cook a finely diced onion in a little oil, then add some chopped garlic, ground cumin, ground coriander and seasoning, along with two 400 g (14 oz) tins of kidney, pinto or black beans, including their soaking liquid, and 250 ml (1 cup) of stock or water. Cook for 15–20 minutes, until the liquid has evaporated. Mash or blend the beans and you're ready to go.

Swaps

Vegan – cheese: vegan cheese or omit

Capsicums – mushrooms, spring onions (scallions), zucchini (courgettes) or cauliflower

Rice – brown rice (add an extra 250 ml/1 cup of stock) or quinoa

Greens on romesco

Serves 4-6 as a side · Vegan · Gluten Free

3 large red capsicums (bell peppers),
cut in half

3 tomatoes, quartered

6–8 garlic cloves, unpeeled

60 ml (¼ cup) olive oil,
plus extra for drizzling

salt and pepper

100 g (⅔ cup) almonds

1 tbsp apple cider vinegar

2 tsp smoky paprika

¼ tsp cayenne pepper (optional)

2 bunches of broccolini, chopped in
half lengthways

200 g (7 oz) sugar snap peas,
stringy part removed

juice of ½ lemon

basil leaves, to serve

Swaps

*Broccolini and sugar snap peas – kale,
broccoli, green beans, broad (fava)
beans, zucchini (courgettes), cabbage
or asparagus*

This is such an unsuspecting but beautiful way to turn a few soggy capsicums into a spectacular and very easy vegetable main. It's a pretty hands-off meal, with your oven doing most of the work. If you can get hold of a heap of cheap capsicums, I suggest doubling the romesco recipe and saving half to spread over sandwiches, eat with potatoes or any savoury breakfast for the next week or two. I've used broccolini and sugar snap peas as the 'greens' here, but really whatever vegetables you need to use up would work. It's heavenly scooped onto fresh buttered bread, or served as part of a potluck dinner or feast.

Preheat the oven to 200°C (400°F) fan-forced.

Arrange the capsicums, tomato and garlic in a large baking dish, drizzle with a little olive oil and sprinkle with some salt and pepper. Transfer to the oven and roast for about 1 hour or until the tomato has released lots of juice and looks shrivelled, and the capsicum skins are starting to blacken. Remove the dish from the oven, scatter over the almonds, then continue to bake for another 5–8 minutes, until the almonds are beginning to brown. Watch them carefully, to avoid burning.

Transfer the veggies and almonds to a food processor and leave to cool for 10 minutes. Squeeze the roasted garlic out of their skins and add to the food processor as well.

Pour 80 ml (⅓ cup) of water into the hot baking dish and gently move it around to 'deglaze' the dish, releasing some of the brown semi-burnt bits of tomato (where heaps of flavour is), plus this will make your washing-up job easier. Pour the water and roasty bits into the food processor, along with the vinegar, paprika, cayenne pepper (if using), olive oil and a little salt and pepper. Process the mixture until thick and smooth, then taste and adjust the seasoning if needed.

Heat your largest frying pan over high heat until it's searing hot. Add the broccolini with an extra drizzle of olive oil and cook for about 2 minutes, tossing it just once or twice. Add the sugar snap peas and toss the pan to help them reach the heat. Cook for a further 1–2 minutes, just enough to sear the vegetables without letting them lose their vibrancy and crunch, which will complement the rich and creamy romesco. Season the vegetables well with salt and pepper, then squeeze over the lemon juice and remove from the heat.

Spread the romesco sauce onto a serving plate and arrange the cooked greens on top. Drizzle with some extra olive oil, scatter with basil leaves and serve. ✳

Carrot

Recipes

I always have an eternal oversupply of carrots at the bottom
of the crisper drawer. They're so cheap and accessible all year
round, so we almost always buy a kilo or two when we're at the
shops or markets, only for them to sit for weeks waiting to be
used. In fact, carrots were the vegetable that inspired this book.
They're so often there to add bulk or base to a dish, rather than
the main ingredient that inspires a meal. So in these recipes
carrots aren't an afterthought, they're the feature, and I hope
they inspire you to give those soggy, sad carrots in your fridge
a new life.

With Pip, Grace and Judy

How do you navigate sharing a kitchen?

We like to share dinners together and the occasional lunch when our schedules align. We all have experience living in shared spaces and take responsibility for our own mess – if someone has prepared a meal for the house someone else will take on clean-up duty. One of our challenges is that we have quite a small fridge, so it can be difficult to meal prep or store leftovers.

What's your favourite way to cook/eat carrots?

Pip: Honey carrots cooked in a pan with lots of cinnamon.

Judy: In a curry with sesame, potato and lentils.

Grace: to be honest, I just love to snack on raw carrots!

What do you love about living in a share house generally, or about this house in particular?

What bonds us all together is our love for all that feels warm and cosy. Whether that's through design (mid-century furniture), food, conversations or connection. Our house is a testament to our three unique energies that blend together to create a nurturing and warm home. When we were forced to move out of our last home and into our current one, we knew that we wanted a big yard for Teddy, a kitchen with lots of space and a gas stove, and to live close to the CBD. Those aren't simple demands in the current rental market. Although we feel very lucky to have found a house that fulfils all those requirements, our friendship is what makes this place a home.

What gives you and your housemates hope for a better world?

All three of us love spending time with children and believe that they have a lot to teach us. One time in between our moves, we were collecting packing boxes from a house we found on Marketplace, when we had an interesting conversation with a school-aged child who lived there. He was having a passionate yarn about the number of cars parked on the street when half a dozen bus stops were located so close by. It's a modest example, but one that we shared some joy in knowing that the next generation of thinkers had a grasp on the damaging tendencies of our consumerist society. ✳

Pasta e ceci

Serves 4–6 · Vegan · Gluten Free

60 ml (¼ cup) olive oil, plus extra
for drizzling

500 g (1 lb 2 oz) carrots, finely diced

1 onion, finely diced

2 tbsp rosemary leaves, chopped
(or 2 tsp dried)

2 tsp thyme leaves, chopped
(or 2 tsp dried)

½ long red chilli, finely chopped, plus
extra if needed

8 garlic cloves, finely chopped

2 bay leaves

2 x 400 g (14 oz) tins chickpeas
(garbanzo beans), including their
soaking water

750 ml (3 cups) vegetable stock

salt and pepper

500 g (1 lb 2 oz) small pasta of
your choice (such as orecchiette,
gnocchetti, penne, rigatoni or
a gluten-free equivalent)

juice of 1 lemon

20 g (1 cup) flat-leaf parsley leaves,
roughly chopped

grated parmesan, to serve (optional)

Pasta, simmered directly in a humble but flavoursome and savoury chickpea and carrot soup–like sauce, might not sound like a show-stopper, but everyone I make this dish for is surprised by how much they like it. Plus it's cheap, vegan and easy to make in huge quantities. The chilli is really important in the sauce, so add more if it's not coming through; the same goes for the lemon juice that finishes it all off. Do take care not to overcook the pasta, and don't be tempted to skimp on the recommended cooking time for the carrot and onion.

Heat the olive oil, carrot and onion in a large heavy-based saucepan over low heat. Cook, stirring frequently, for 30–40 minutes, until completely reduced and golden. Don't be tempted to reduce the cooking time, as this caramelisation is essential to the flavour of the dish. Add the rosemary, thyme, chilli and garlic to the pan, then increase the heat a little and stir to combine. Cook for a further 3–4 minutes, until fragrant, then throw in the bay leaves.

Pour the chickpeas and their soaking water, the vegetable stock and 250 ml (1 cup) of water into the pan. Bring the mixture to a gentle boil, then remove from the heat.

Using either a stick blender or a potato masher, crush approximately half the chickpeas and the vegetable mixture, leaving some of it chunky and taking care to avoid the bay leaves. This will thicken the sauce a little, though it will still be a very liquid soup. At this point, season with salt and pepper, then taste and add more salt or chilli, as needed.

Return the pan to medium heat, bring the soup to a simmer, then add the pasta and cook, stirring frequently, for 2–3 minutes less than the packet instructions, adding more water if necessary. Remove the pan from the heat – the pasta will continue to cook as it cools and this prevents the dish from becoming gluggy.

Squeeze over the lemon juice and toss to combine. Taste the mixture and add some final seasoning if required. Before serving, sprinkle over the chopped parsley, along with some extra olive oil and freshly ground black pepper. Serve with grated parmesan, if you like. ✳

Golden carrot falafels with hummus & flatbreads

Serves 4–6 · Vegan

295 g (1⅓ cups) dried chickpeas (garbanzo beans)

4 carrots, roughly chopped

2 tsp ground coriander

2 tsp ground sumac

1 heaped tsp ground turmeric

1 heaped tsp salt

bunch of chopped soft herbs (any or a combination of mint, coriander/cilantro, dill or flat-leaf parsley)

½ brown onion, roughly chopped

3 garlic cloves, peeled

juice of 1 lemon

80 ml (⅓ cup) olive oil

3 tbsp plain (all-purpose) flour

1 tsp baking powder

1–2 litres (34–68 fl oz) vegetable oil (or another neutral oil), for deep-frying

salad and pickles, to serve

Flatbreads

310 ml (1¼ cups) warm water

1 heaped tsp instant dried yeast

1 tbsp honey or maple syrup

500 g (3⅓ cups) plain (all-purpose) flour, plus extra if needed and for dusting

2 tbsp olive oil, plus extra for drizzling

1 heaped tsp salt

Ground turmeric, alongside roasted carrots, gives these falafel their sunshine yellow hue, while the bright flavour comes from the addition of lemon and sumac. The falafel mix can be made ahead and stored in the fridge for a couple of days, ready to be fried up and devoured fresh, as all falafel must. I've included recipes for hummus and flatbreads, because I almost always make all three together. So basically this is three recipes in one – give it a good read before you start preparing, as you'll want to adjust the steps and timings depending on what bits you're making.

Place all the chickpeas (2⅔ cups in total, if making both the falafels and hummus) in a large saucepan or bowl and cover with 2 litres (68 fl oz) of water. Leave to soak at room temperature for at least 5–6 hours, or up to 24 hours – though in the fridge is best if it's a warm day.

Preheat the oven to 200°C (400°F) fan-forced.

Place the carrot on a baking tray, transfer to the oven and roast for 30–40 minutes, until a little softened and turning brown. Leave to cool. This step can be done up to a few days ahead, whenever you've got something else cooking in the oven.

Meanwhile, prepare the flatbreads by mixing the warm water, yeast and honey together in a large bowl. Set aside for 10 minutes, or until the mixture is foamy. Add the flour, olive oil and salt and mix well to combine. Knead the dough for 5 minutes, adding a little extra flour if it's sticking to your hands, until it's smooth and stretchy. You could also do this in a stand mixer fitted with a dough hook if you prefer. Drizzle over a little olive oil, cover the bowl and leave the dough to rise for about 1 hour, until doubled in size.

To prepare the hummus, add half the soaked chickpeas, 1.5 litres (51 fl oz) of water, a generous pinch of salt and the bicarbonate of soda to a large saucepan. Bring to the boil, then reduce the heat to a simmer and cook, skimming any foam that rises to the surface, for about 30 minutes, until the chickpeas are soft and the skins have peeled away. Drain the chickpeas and discard as many of the skins as you can (don't worry about getting them all, you will go insane – just remove the obvious ones or those that have clumped together). Leave the chickpeas to cool a little, then transfer to a food processor and add the lemon juice, tahini, oil, salt, garlic and sumac. Blitz on high speed until smooth, then taste the hummus and adjust the seasoning to your preference. Blitz again, slowly drizzling in the ice-cold water. This thins the hummus out a little and helps it to become super light. Pour the hummus into a bowl, drizzle over a little extra olive oil and sumac.

Dust a clean work surface with flour and tip the rested dough onto it. Cut the dough into 6–8 pieces and set aside to relax again for a few minutes. Roll or stretch each piece of dough into a thin, roundish flatbread, getting it as thin as you can or at least 15–20 cm (6–8 in) in diameter. →

Hummus

295 g (1⅓ cups) dried chickpeas

1 tsp bicarbonate of soda
(baking soda)

juice of 1 lemon

65 g (¼ cup) tahini

60 ml (¼ cup) olive oil, plus extra
for drizzling

1 tsp salt

2 garlic cloves, peeled

1 tsp ground sumac, plus extra to serve

60 ml (¼ cup) ice-cold water

Swaps

*Carrots – pumpkin or capsicum
(bell peppers)*

Heat a heavy-based frying pan over high heat, then, working in batches, cook the flatbreads for 1 minute each side – don't let them get too brown or they'll become crunchy and you won't be able to roll up your falafel. This is a good task to get a housemate to help with, so one of you can stretch and roll the dough, as the other cooks. The flatbreads can also be made ahead of time and kept in an airtight container. Re-warm in the oven before serving.

To make the falafels, drain and rinse the remaining chickpeas, then transfer to the large bowl of a food processor, along with the roasted carrot, spices, salt, herbs, onion, garlic, lemon juice and olive oil. Blend until the chickpeas are almost smooth and the mixture is a thick, grainy paste. Add the flour and baking powder and stir or blitz well. Taste the mixture and add more salt or lemon if needed. Set the mixture aside in the fridge until you're ready to cook – the mixture will keep in the fridge for up to 2 days.

To cook the falafels, heat 3 cm (1¼ in) of vegetable oil in a heavy-based saucepan over medium–high heat. Test the oil is hot enough by adding a small teaspoon of the falafel mix; if it immediately sizzles it's hot enough. Roll tablespoons of the falafel mix into small balls, then, working in batches and making sure you don't overcrowd the pan, lower them into the hot oil and cook for 2–3 minutes each side until they're deep brown. Remove the falafels from the oil and drain on paper towel.

Serve the falafels and flatbread warm, alongside the hummus and some salad and pickles. The leftovers are great for a couple of days, and make a fantastic packed lunch. ✳

Roasted carrots, olives & currants with homemade labneh

Serves 4–6 as a side · Gluten Free

2 bunches of Dutch (baby) carrots, sliced or cut into pieces

80 ml (⅓ cup) olive oil, plus extra for drizzling

salt and pepper

2 tsp fennel seeds

120 g (¾ cup) pitted olives of your choice

75 g (½ cup) currants

Labneh

750 g (3 cups) Greek-style yoghurt

1 tsp salt

Swaps

Vegan – yoghurt: coconut yoghurt, plus 60–80 ml (¼–⅓ cup) fresh lemon juice

Carrots – pumpkin (winter squash), eggplant (aubergine) or brussels sprouts (or any other roasting vegetables)

This dish makes a beautiful side, or potluck addition, and would be great as a starter or snack served with some bread. The luscious, silky homemade labneh pairs terrifically with the sweet roasted carrots, olives and currants. Making your own labneh is incredibly easy, provided you have some muslin, or a good substitute, handy. Coffee filters, a new/clean chux cloth or a thin tea towel are my go-tos. Just ensure that you use good-quality, natural Greek-style yoghurt and leave it to drain for at least 5–6 hours, but ideally overnight. If you're making this dish on a whim and don't have that time to spare, store-bought labneh or even just salted yoghurt make perfectly good substitutes. I like using a couple of bunches of baby carrots in this dish, but you can use regular carrots, sliced either into chunky discs or sticks.

To make the labneh, combine the yoghurt and salt in a bowl. Line a small bowl with a large square of muslin (cheesecloth), new chux cloth, thin, clean tea towel or an extra-large coffee filter. Place the salted yoghurt in the middle, then fold up the sides and use a rubber band to tightly capture the yoghurt in a ball. If using coffee filters and they aren't quite big enough, split the yoghurt into 2–3 batches. The next step is to drain the wrapped yoghurt for at least 5–6 hours, and up to overnight. If you're in a cool place, this is best done by hanging the ball from a wooden spoon over a bowl in the sink, to catch the whey. If it's warmer, rest the ball in a strainer or colander rested over a bowl in the fridge, ensuring that the ball isn't sitting in the liquid.

When the labneh is ready, preheat the oven to 200°C (400°F) fan-forced.

Spread the carrot over a large baking tray and add the olive oil. Sprinkle over some salt and pepper and toss well to coat. Roast the carrot for 25 minutes or until beginning to turn golden. Add the fennel seeds, olives and currants to the tray, tossing them with the carrot. Return the tray to the oven for a further 20 minutes, or until the carrot is beginning to shrivel and the currants and olives are blistered.

Gently remove the labneh from the cloth; depending on how long you've drained it, it will range from a dollop-cream consistency, up to a thick cream cheese. Spread the labneh across a large plate or serving dish. (Save the whey to use as you would buttermilk or milk in baked goods or savoury dishes.) Use tongs to arrange the carrot mixture over the labneh. Finish with an extra drizzle of olive oil and serve. ✳

Carrot mac 'n' cheese with crunchy cheese crumbs

Serves 4–6

4 large carrots, diced

1 large brown onion, diced

50 g (1¾ oz) salted butter

6 garlic cloves, roughly chopped

2 tbsp dijon mustard

½ tsp nutmeg (ideally freshly grated)

2 heaped tsp smoky paprika

3 tbsp plain (all-purpose) flour

500 ml (2 cups) milk

salt and pepper

500 ml (2 cups) vegetable stock

500 g (1 lb 2 oz) macaroni (or another small pasta shape)

100 g (1 cup) grated vintage cheddar

50 g (½ cup) grated parmesan

Crunchy cheese crumbs

100 g (1 cup) grated cheddar

Swaps

Gluten free – plain (all-purpose) flour, pasta and bread: gluten-free alternatives

Vegan – butter: vegan margarine; milk: plant-based milk; cheese: vegan cheese or nutritional yeast; cheese crumbs: toasted breadcrumbs

When I was a kid, packet Kraft Mac 'n' Cheese was the stuff of my dreams. Even though this recipe is obviously far from it, there's something about its simple savouriness that feels reminiscent. Not to mention the bright-orange colour hit from all those carrots. This mac 'n' cheese hits all those comfort-food notes, perfect on a cold evening or a slow, hungover day requiring carbs and salt aplenty. It's really easy to whack together, so long as you have a decent blender to get that silky sauce effect. The crunchy cheese pieces on top are optional, but a fun and easy way to add some texture, and a fun trick for your tool kit (they're great over roasted veggies and salads).

Place the carrot, onion and butter in a large, heavy-based saucepan over medium heat and gently cook, stirring frequently, for 15–20 minutes, until the vegetables are softened with some golden edges. Add the garlic and cook for another few minutes, until fragrant.

As the vegetables cook, prepare the crunchy cheese crumbs. Heat a large, non-stick frying pan over medium heat until very hot, then scatter a small handful of the grated cheese across the pan. As the cheese melts, it will form a lacy disc. Cook for 1–2 minutes, watching it carefully, until the oil starts to separate and the cheese begins to turn golden brown. Flip over the melted cheese disc, using a spatula or tongs, and cook for another 30 seconds or until golden, then transfer to a board or a plate to cool. Repeat with the remaining cheese. Once the cheese cools, it will crisp up again – break the discs into shards or small crumbs.

Add the mustard, nutmeg, paprika and flour to the pan with the carrot and stir really well to coat. As the flour mixes with the buttery vegetables, it will become gluggy, which is what we're looking for. After a minute or so, pour in the milk and stir for about 5 minutes, until it forms a chunky bechamel sauce.

Remove the pan from the heat and transfer the mixture to a high-powered blender, then blitz until smooth. Alternatively you can use a stick blender to whiz the mixture until silky. Season well with salt and pepper.

Return the sauce to the pan and stir through 500 ml (2 cups) of water and the stock. Heat the sauce until bubbles begin to form around the edge of the pan, then add the macaroni. Cook the macaroni for a few minutes less than the packet directions, stirring it often to stop it sticking to the base of the pan. Small pasta cooks quickly, and will continue to soften as it cools, so it's better to undercook it slightly. Remove the pan from the heat and stir through the grated parmesan. Taste and season well.

Divide the macaroni cheese among bowls, topping each with a sprinkling of the crunchy cheese crumbs. ✳

Walnut & lentil burgers with carrot jam & vegan aioli

Serves 6–8 · Vegan

95 g (½ cup) couscous

100 g (1 cup) walnuts

2 x 400 g (14 oz) tins lentils, rinsed (reserve 125 ml/½ cup of the liquid for the aioli)

½ onion, roughly chopped

1 carrot, roughly chopped

1 tsp dried thyme (or 1 tbsp thyme leaves)

1 heaped tsp smoky paprika

salt and pepper

75 g (½ cup) plain (all-purpose) flour

vegetable oil (or another neutral oil), for shallow frying

Carrot jam

1 tsp cumin seeds

1 tsp mustard seeds

140 g (⅔ cup) granulated sugar

60 ml (¼ cup) apple cider vinegar

½ tsp salt

4–5 carrots, grated (about 3 loosely packed cups)

Vegan aioli

125 ml (½ cup) liquid from the lentil tins

80 ml (⅓ cup) apple cider vinegar

1 tbsp dijon mustard

2 garlic cloves, peeled

½ tsp white pepper

½ tsp salt

375 ml (1 ½ cups) vegetable oil (or another neutral oil)

I like to serve these burgers with a platter of thinly sliced salad vegetables, cheese and pickles or jalapenos, ready for people to assemble their own bun. The carrot jam is such a fun way to use up a bunch of carrots; it's delicious, vibrant and super easy. The recipes for both the carrot jam and vegan aioli will make at least double of what you need for this meal, so store the leftovers in jars in the fridge to eat with just about everything and anything for up to a couple of weeks. You can also make all the elements of these burgers ahead of time, and simply reheat the patties before serving.

Start with the carrot jam. Whisk the ingredients, except the carrots, along with 375 ml (1½ cups) of water, in a saucepan to combine. Add the grated carrot and stir, then push the carrot down so it's completely submerged in the liquid. Place the saucepan over medium–low heat and cook for about 1 hour, returning to the jam occasionally to stir and push the carrot down again. The jam is ready when most of the liquid has evaporated, but you can still push down the carrot and some bright-orange liquid remains. Transfer half the jam to a bowl, to serve, and the rest to a jar to store in the fridge, ensuring that you distribute the remaining liquid evenly between the two. Store in the fridge to cool until ready to serve.

Next prepare the patties. Rehydrate the couscous according to the packet instructions in a large mixing bowl. Blitz the remaining ingredients except the flour and oil in a food processor until the carrot and onion are finely chopped and the lentils are mostly paste-like. Transfer everything to the bowl with the couscous and stir to combine well, adding a generous seasoning of salt and pepper. Add the flour and stir to evenly distribute, but don't worry about mixing it in completely, some little remaining streaks are fine.

Roll the burger mixture into 6–8 balls, then use your hands to flatten the balls into thick, tight patties, to ensure they won't break up when frying.

Heat 2–3 tablespoons of vegetable oil in a large frying pan over medium heat. Working in batches, cook the patties for 2 minutes each side or until cooked through and golden. Repeat with the remaining patties, adding more oil as needed.

To prepare the vegan aioli, place the ingredients except the oil in a food processor or blender. Blitz for a few seconds to combine, then very slowly trickle in the oil in a steady stream while blending. This should take 1–2 minutes, and towards the end you'll notice it begin to thicken. Once all the oil is added, taste the aioli and adjust the seasoning if needed. Depending on how quickly you added your oil and the type of blender you're using it won't be quite as thick as store-bought aioli, but you can continue adding more oil to get it there if you like. You can also make the aioli in a bowl with a hand whisk – just crush the garlic well beforehand, or use garlic powder or roasted garlic instead, and note that you might not get as thick an aioli.

Serve the burgers, carrot jam and aioli with the buns and salad toppings. ✳

<u>To serve</u>

6–8 burger buns

sliced salad toppings (I use tomato, red onion, lettuce, pickles and avocado)

Swaps

Gluten free – couscous: 185 g (1 cup) cooked brown rice, added to the blender; plain (all-purpose) flour: cornflour (corn starch)

Carrot & pistachio muffins with cheesecake topping

Makes 12 · Gluten Free

100 g (3 ½ oz) unsalted butter, softened

95 g (½ cup) brown sugar

1 tsp vanilla essence

2 eggs

170 ml (⅔ cup) milk

235 g (1½ cups) finely grated carrot

½ tsp ground allspice

1 tsp ground cinnamon

75 g (½ cup) shelled pistachios, chopped, plus extra to serve

225 g (1 ½ cups) self-raising flour (or use gluten-free self-raising flour)

Cheesecake topping

250 g (1 cup) cream cheese, softened

1 egg

1 tsp vanilla essence

115 g (½ cup) caster (superfine) sugar

These muffins make the best afternoon tea or snack to share with friends or workmates, and you could make a single cake if you prefer. I love the lightly spiced batter, which is made all the more interesting with the addition of pistachios. The cheesecake top works somewhat like a cream-cheese icing, adding some creaminess and change of texture. You could blitz the pistachios in a food processor to save chopping them, though I really like them to be a mixture of sizes – some fine like powder, but other pieces large enough to provide a little crunch.

Heat the oven to 180°C (350°F) fan-forced. Line or grease a 12-hole muffin tin.

To make the cheesecake topping, use electric beaters to beat the soft cream cheese, egg, vanilla and sugar together until smooth and silky. Set aside in the fridge until ready to use.

In a large bowl, beat together the butter and sugar until light and fluffy. Add the vanilla and eggs and beat well until the mixture is pale. Add the milk and carrot and stir well to combine. If your milk and/or carrots were cold from the fridge, the mixture will probably split here and look rather putrid, but don't worry, it'll come back together in a moment.

In a separate small bowl, mix together the spices, pistachios and flour, then add this to the carrot mixture and gently fold until combined. Don't be tempted to mix vigorously here.

Scoop the carrot mixture into the prepared muffin tin holes, then use the back of a spoon to press an indent into each portion of batter. Scoop a large tablespoon of the cheesecake mixture into each indent, then sprinkle with a few extra pistachio pieces. Bake for 20–25 minutes, until the cheesecake tops are just beginning to crack and the muffins have risen and spring back a little when touched.

Serve the muffins warm, and store any leftovers for a couple of days in an airtight container at room temperature. ✳

Cauliflower

As well as having their own lovely flavour, cauliflowers are a sponge, soaking up the flavour of ingredients cooked around them. They make a beautiful vegetable centrepiece and are adaptable to cook in many different cuisines, as you'll see in this chapter, which features cauliflower dishes inspired by Chinese, Italian, Moroccan and Middle-Eastern cooking. They're also an awesome substitute in most dishes that call for mince because of their hearty texture and bulk; in fact, I urge you to make the ragout in this chapter and serve it to an unsuspecting meat eater; they may not even realise it's packed with cauliflower. All of the recipes here use the whole cauliflower, you can even cook the leaves.

With Megan, Imogen, Josa and Misha

Describe your household

Imogen is a musician who plays in a handful of local bands, and does guitar, sound, and tour tech work in between day jobs. Meg is a photographer and graphic designer who hates talking about themselves. They play basketball quite badly, but with enthusiasm. Misha is a disability support worker who loves to volunteer on community projects, cooks, reads and goes for long walks with Buster. Buster is Misha and Meg's energetic child/dog who they take amazing care of, including twice daily walks. Buster repays them by trying to drag whole branches home as souvenirs. Our chicken, The Lady, is the matriarch of the house and has been here the longest. Josa is a published author and carer of adorable baby possums. They need to be fed every four hours. Josa, and the possums. Josa also makes a banging cocktail and regularly cooks delicious meals for the fam.

Meg and Misha have been here for years, since various election campaigns for The Greens were being run (and won!) out of the living room. Imogen moved in just over a year ago, and Josa most recently. Both have brought the energy that makes it the cosy queer nest it is today.

How do you navigate sharing a kitchen?

Never touch someone's leftovers. Everything else is negotiable. Josa thinks leftovers are negotiable too ... Sometimes fridge space becomes an issue – we've all become masters of fridge-Tetris over our time living in various share houses, so it's not a huge deal. Like many share houses, we sometimes have forgotten specimens festering in the back of the fridge. Throwing those out sure does create more room for those five soy and oat milk cartons!

Mish experiments with different vegetables to create delicious plant-based eats for us to pick at. Tofu is ever-present in our fridge and miso eggplant is a fan-favourite, at least for Josa!

What's your favourite way to cook/eat cauliflower?

We love a classic cauliflower bake. It doesn't get more comforting and homely than that! Also roasted cauliflower or cauliflower wings.

What do you love about living in this house?

Living in a queer share house is great, especially one like this that comes with a dog, cat and chickens. It's a kind and nurturing household, and we all make an effort to be supportive of each other, which makes our house feel homely. *

Cauliflower & four-cheese lasagne

Serves 4–8

800 g (1 lb 12 oz) cauliflower (about 2 heads), leaves and stalks included, roughly chopped into bite-sized florets

80 ml (⅓ cup) olive oil, plus extra for drizzling

salt and pepper

75 g (2¾ oz) salted butter

1 onion, diced

5 garlic cloves, minced

3 tbsp plain (all-purpose) flour

½ tsp nutmeg (ideally freshly grated)

1 tsp white pepper

1 x 400 g (14 oz) tin cannellini beans, including soaking liquid

625 ml (2½ cups) milk

500 ml (2 cups) vegetable stock

150 g (5½ oz) cream cheese, chopped

150 g (1½ cups) grated vintage cheddar

100 g (1 cup) grated parmesan

125 g (4½ oz) fresh mozzarella, thinly sliced (keep the whey from the tub)

375 g (13 oz) fresh lasagne sheets (or dried sheets, soaked in hot water for 10 minutes before using)

generous handful of sage leaves

For a lasagne with four different cheeses, butter and a lot of milk, this dish isn't actually as rich as it might sound. The dairy is distributed among two entire cauliflowers and some hidden cannellini beans for protein and extra substance. The result is a super-creamy and luscious lasagne that makes a perfect centrepiece at a feast, or an easy meal to feel a big crowd (with serious leftovers potential). If a more traditional tomato-based lasagne is already firmly in your repertoire, give this one a go. Not only is it incredibly yum, it might open your eyes to a world of new lasagne possibilities.

Preheat the oven to 200°C (400°F) fan-forced. Line a large baking tray with baking paper.

Spread about half the cauliflower florets across the prepared tray, drizzle with the olive oil and sprinkle over some salt and pepper. Roast the cauliflower for about 25 minutes, tossing it halfway through cooking, until golden brown and shrivelled.

Meanwhile, melt the butter in a large saucepan over medium heat until starting to brown. Add the onion and cook for 5–10 minutes, until soft and starting to caramelise. Add the remaining cauliflower florets and toss them through the onion and butter. Cook for 5–10 minutes, until the cauliflower has softened a bit and is beginning to reduce in size. Add the garlic and toss it through the mixture, giving it a couple of minutes to cook. Add the flour and toss well to coat the ingredients, then cook for a couple of minutes. Add the nutmeg, white pepper, cannellini beans and their soaking liquid and milk, and stir the mixture really well, making sure the ingredients don't catch on the base of the pan. Cook for about 5 minutes, until the sauce is starting to thicken, then add the vegetable stock and stir through well. At this point, either transfer the mixture to a food processor or (much easier) use a stick blender to pulse the mixture to a thick white sauce. Don't worry about getting everything super smooth; a bit of texture and some chunks of cauliflower are really nice in the lasagne.

Add the cream cheese and most of the cheddar and parmesan to the pan, reserving a handful of each for the topping. Stir the cheeses into the sauce, until they've melted through completely. Taste the sauce and adjust the seasoning if required. Finally, stir through the mozzarella whey. If you don't have the whey, just add an additional 125 ml (½ cup) of milk or stock instead. Your sauce should be quite liquidy and look like a slightly chunky cauliflower soup. As it cooks in the lasagne, the liquid will thicken further and be soaked up by the lasagne sheets.

Swaps

Vegan – butter: olive oil; milk: plant-based milk; cheese: vegan cheese, cashew cheese and/or nutritional yeast

Gluten free – plain (all-purpose) flour: cornflour (corn starch); lasagne sheets: gluten-free lasagne sheets, slices of zucchini (courgette) or par-cooked potato

Cauliflower – broccoli, mushrooms or pumpkin

To assemble the lasagne, dollop about 1 tablespoon of the cauliflower sauce into a large baking dish and spread it out. Place a layer of lasagne sheets on top, then cover with about one-third of the remaining cauliflower sauce. Add half the roasted cauliflower, followed by another layer of lasagne sheets, another one-third of the sauce and the remaining roasted cauliflower. Finish with a final layer of lasagne sheets and the remaining sauce, and scatter over the reserved cheddar and parmesan.

Transfer the lasagne to the oven and bake for 15 minutes, until the cheese on top is melted and the sauce is beginning to bubble up. Remove from the oven and scatter over the sliced mozzarella, then spread the sage leaves evenly over the top and drizzle with a little extra olive oil. Return to the oven for a final 15–20 minutes, until the cheese is golden and the sage leaves are crisp.

Allow the lasagne to rest on your work surface for 15 minutes before serving. The leftovers will be excellent for a few days, stored in an airtight container in the fridge. ✳

Whole roasted cauliflower with harissa marinade & almond crust

Serves 6–8 · Vegan · Gluten Free

2 tbsp harissa paste

125 ml (½ cup) olive oil, plus extra for drizzling

1 tbsp honey or maple syrup

1 tsp ground cumin

1 tsp ground coriander

1 tsp salt

1 large head of cauliflower, leaves included

185 ml (¾ cup) vegetable stock

handful of fresh herbs, such as parsley, mint, dill, chives or thyme, to serve

Almond crust

80 g (½ cup) almonds

30 g (¼ cup) pumpkin seeds (pepitas)

1 tbsp cumin seeds

1 tbsp coriander seeds

½ tsp salt

This whole cauliflower makes a beautiful centrepiece as part of a big spread, or an easy hands-off main for dinner, served with some flatbread, hummus and salad. The slightly sweet and spicy harissa marinade will drip off the cauliflower a little as it cooks, and the sauce that collects at the bottom is beautiful poured over the finished dish. Unlike other roasted cauliflower recipes, this one isn't about charred, gnarly pieces. It's cooked slow and covered, with the results yielding super-tender, melt-in-your-mouth cauliflower that can be pulled apart in a similar way to a tender roast lamb or brisket.

Preheat the oven to 200°C (400°F) fan-forced.

Whisk the harissa, olive oil, honey or maple syrup, cumin, coriander and salt together in a small bowl. Place the cauliflower in your largest ovenproof dish and pour in the vegetable stock.

Drizzle over most of the harissa marinade, reserving about 2 tablespoons to use later. Use your hands to rub the marinade into the cauliflower, ensuring that you coat all of it, including the base and the leaves. Cover the dish with a lid or foil, then transfer to the oven and roast for 1 hour.

Meanwhile, blitz the almond crust ingredients in a food processor to form a rough dukkah-like mix. You can chop the nuts and pound the seeds and leave it a bit chunkier if you don't have a food processor. Set aside.

Remove the cauliflower from the oven and drizzle over the reserved marinade. Scatter most of the almond crust mix on top of the cauliflower, using the back of a spoon to gently press it onto the crown to create a thick crust, taking care not to touch the super-hot dish. Scatter the remaining almond mix around the sides and drizzle with a little extra olive oil. Return to the oven, uncovered, and roast for another 25–30 minutes, until the cauliflower is soft and the almond crust is crispy and golden.

Carefully transfer the cauliflower to a serving dish, ready to carve. Serve hot or warm with the leftover sauce from the bottom of the pan, topped with some extra olive oil and a scattering of fresh herbs. ✳

Fried cauliflower karaage with wasabi slaw

Serves 4–6 · Vegan · Gluten Free

125 ml (½ cup) soy sauce or tamari

80 ml (⅓ cup) cooking sake

1 tbsp tahini

2 tsp wasabi paste

1 tsp ground cinnamon

3 garlic cloves, finely grated

1 tbsp finely grated or minced ginger

2 tbsp maple syrup

250 g (2 cups) potato starch, plus extra if needed

1 large head of cauliflower, broken into bite-sized florets

vegetable oil (or another neutral oil), for deep-frying

1 tsp garlic powder

1 tsp salt

1 tsp white pepper

Wasabi slaw

225 g (3 cups) finely shredded white cabbage

2 carrots, grated

3 spring onions (scallions), finely chopped

1 large apple, grated

125 g (½ cup) vegan mayonnaise (vegan Kewpie is ideal)

2 tbsp soy sauce or tamari

2 tbsp rice wine vinegar

2 tsp wasabi paste

1 tbsp sesame oil

salt and white pepper

1 tbsp toasted sesame seeds (optional)

Karaage chicken is definitely one of my favourite meat dishes, and no, this adaptation doesn't taste 'just like' the delicious Japanese classic. It does have a striking resemblance though, and is perfect to enjoy on a warm afternoon alongside a cold beer in just the same way. If you don't want to make the slaw to serve with it, I do recommend mixing a little dipping sauce from the dressing ingredients – Kewpie, soy sauce and wasabi – and eating the fried nuggets with some pickles alongside. Heaven. I like to keep the pieces of cauliflower pretty small – large bite-sized is perfect for an ideal batter ratio, but it doesn't matter if the pieces aren't uniform. When doing your final coat in the starch, make sure you really get it onto the florets, to increase the crispiness of the cauliflower. Potato starch is easy to find in any Asian supermarket. Alternatively, substitute with cornflour.

In a large bowl, whisk together the soy sauce or tamari, sake, tahini, wasabi, cinnamon, garlic, ginger and maple syrup to form a thick sauce, ensuring that the wasabi hasn't clumped together and is mixed through well. Add 60 g (½ cup) of the potato starch and whisk it through, crushing any clumps that form. Add the cauliflower and use your hands to coat each piece thoroughly in the thick marinade. Cover the bowl with a tea towel and marinate in the fridge for at least 30 minutes, but ideally longer – up to 24 hours.

Shortly before you're ready to cook the cauliflower, prepare the wasabi slaw. Place the vegetables and apple in a large salad bowl and toss well to combine. In a separate bowl, whisk together the mayonnaise, soy sauce or tamari, rice wine vinegar, wasabi and sesame oil, and season with a pinch of salt and white pepper. Drizzle the dressing over the slaw ingredients just before you're ready to serve, using tongs to combine well.

Heat a deep frying pan over medium heat with enough vegetable oil to half submerge your largest piece of cauliflower. As the oil heats, prepare a bowl with the remaining potato starch, the garlic powder, salt and white pepper, mixing well to combine. Remove the marinated cauliflower from the fridge and give it a good mix, taking care to coat it again with any marinade that has collected at the bottom of the bowl.

Once the oil is screaming hot (test with a small piece of cauliflower – if it sizzles right away, the oil is ready), progressively dunk the cauliflower pieces into the potato starch mixture, moving them around to thoroughly coat, then gently drop into the hot oil and cook, in batches, for 1–2 minutes each side. Transfer the fried cauliflower to a plate lined with paper towel to drain – essential for that crispy finish. Continue until all the cauliflower is cooked, topping up the potato starch mixture if you begin to run out.

Serve the cauliflower karaage alongside the slaw, with lemon wedges and pickles. You could also serve this with some edamame beans and steamed rice, or load the cauliflower, slaw and pickles into a soft bread roll for a delicious burger. ✳

To serve

lemon wedges

pickles of your choice

Swaps

Cabbage or carrot – shredded kohlrabi, brussels sprouts, celery, iceberg lettuce or kale

Cooking sake – Shaoxing rice wine, mirin or rice wine vinegar

Potato starch – cornflour (corn starch)

Wasabi – horseradish cream or hot mustard

Sticky sesame cauliflower with noodles & herby salad

Serves 4–6 • Vegan • Gluten Free

3 tbsp sesame seeds

3 tsp Chinese five spice

2 tsp smoky paprika

60 ml (¼ cup) olive oil

2 tsp brown sugar

2 tbsp soy sauce or tamari

500 g (1 lb 2 oz) cauliflower (about 1 large head), chopped into small 2 cm (¾ in) chunks

40 g (¼ cup) roasted peanut halves

Herby salad

2 tsp sesame oil

1 tbsp rice wine vinegar

salt and pepper

3 small cucumbers or 1 large, sliced into shards on the diagonal

200 g (7 oz) thick 'pad Thai' rice noodles

bunch of coriander (cilantro), leaves picked

bunch of mint, leaves picked

½ red onion, thinly sliced

¼ white cabbage, shredded

Dressing

60 ml (¼ cup) vegan fish sauce

juice of 2 small limes

1 tbsp brown sugar

2 garlic cloves, finely chopped

½ bird's eye chilli, finely chopped (optional)

When you want to feast on something fresh and light but packed full of flavour, this is a perfect dish. Far from a traditional Thai larb, with no pork, or ground sticky rice, it is still reminiscent of this famous salad – and craving it inspired me to make this for the first time. And with quick-pickled cucumbers, shredded cabbage and dressed rice noodles, it's such a wonderful and healthy meal. Pre-mixed 'Chinese five spice' is a cheat's addition to the cauliflower, but you can make up your own with star anise, cloves, cinnamon, fennel and pepper (or as many of these spices as you have) if you don't have a jar of the stuff on the go.

Preheat the oven to 200°C (400°F) fan-forced. Line a large baking tray with baking paper.

In a small bowl, mix together the sesame seeds, spices, olive oil, sugar and soy sauce or tamari to form a thick paste. Spread the cauliflower across the prepared tray and dollop the marinade over the top. Use your hands to toss the cauliflower and coat it in the mixture. Transfer to the oven and bake for 20–30 minutes, turning the cauliflower halfway through cooking, until starting to char and the pieces have shrunk to about one-third of their original size. Add the peanuts to the tray and toss well. Return to the oven for a final 5 minutes, to warm the nuts.

Meanwhile, to make the herby salad, combine the sesame oil, rice wine vinegar and a generous pinch of salt and pepper in a bowl. Add the cucumber and toss to coat, then set aside to pickle until ready to serve.

In a separate bowl, whisk together the dressing ingredients and 80 ml (⅓ cup) of water and set aside.

Cook the noodles according to the packet directions, then drain under cool running water to prevent the noodles becoming gluggy. Toss the noodles with the herbs and onion, along with about half the dressing. Transfer to a serving bowl and top with the warm cauliflower, cabbage and quick-pickled cucumber. Drizzle the remaining dressing over the top and serve. ✳

Cauliflower, pickles & rice salad with creamy herb sauce

Serves 4–6 as a main, or 10–12 as a side · Vegan · Gluten Free

1 large head of cauliflower, chopped into florets

2 tbsp olive oil

salt and pepper

400 g (2 cups) long-grain or jasmine rice

1 tsp ground turmeric

100 g (⅔ cup) almonds, chopped

2 tsp cumin seeds

125 ml (½ cup) pickle juice (from a pickle jar)

85 g (⅔ cup) pitted olives, cut into small dice

3–4 radishes, cut into small dice

80 g (2¾ oz) dill pickles, cut into small dice

3–4 handfuls of mixed leafy herbs, roughly chopped

Creamy herb sauce

2 spring onions (scallions), roughly chopped

large bunch of mixed leafy herbs

2 tbsp tahini

1–2 garlic cloves, peeled

juice of 1 lemon

2 tbsp olive oil

1 long green chilli (optional)

salt and pepper

Swaps

Cauliflower – zucchini (courgette), mushrooms, capsicum (bell pepper), pumpkin (winter squash) or any vegetable that likes being roasted

This hearty salad is vibrant both to look at and to eat. Pickle juice makes an unsuspectedly delicious and simple dressing for this warm rice salad, and the various textures of the finely diced ingredients make this delightful to eat. The herby sauce on top is very flexible and a staple that I make all the time, especially when I find those gloriously enormous bunches of herbs for cheap at the markets. It's a great way to preserve your herbs and add a delicious whack of green to heaps of different meals, so double the mix if you have herbs to use up. Use whatever herbs you have on hand, and save some for tossing through the salad. This dish is substantial enough to serve as a main, or it makes a lovely side alongside some falafel (see page 103) or lentil and walnut patties (see page 112).

Preheat the oven to 200°C (400°F) fan-forced.

Spread the cauliflower in a large baking dish, drizzle over the olive oil and sprinkle with salt and pepper. Roast for 30 minutes, turning the cauliflower halfway through cooking, or until well roasted, with some nice crispy bits. Remove from the oven and set aside.

Meanwhile, rinse the rice well for a couple of minutes under cold running water to remove some of the starchiness. Transfer to a saucepan or rice cooker and add 750 ml (3 cups) of water, the turmeric and a sprinkle of salt and pepper. Bring to the boil, then reduce the heat to a simmer and cook the rice for 12–15 minutes, until the water has evaporated and the rice is just cooked.

As the rice cooks, prepare the creamy herb sauce by blending all the ingredients and 3 tablespoons of water until smooth. Taste the sauce and ensure you season it well – without enough salt it will taste very bland.

In a small frying pan over low heat, toast the almonds and cumin seeds for 3–4 minutes, until browned. Alternatively toast the almonds in the oven while the cauliflower roasts. Season with a little salt.

Place the warm rice in a large serving bowl, drizzle over the pickle juice and toss well to coat. Add the olives, radish, pickles, herbs and roasted cauliflower and gently stir to combine. Spoon over the herby sauce, and scatter with the toasted almonds and cumin seeds just before serving. ✳

Rich cauliflower & walnut ragout with silky polenta

Serves 4–6 · Gluten Free

170 ml (⅔ cup) olive oil

1 onion, diced

2 carrots, diced

5 garlic cloves, minced

150 g (5½ oz) tomato paste (concentrated purée)

65 g (⅔ cup) walnuts, finely chopped

1 tsp dried oregano

1 tsp dried basil

2 tsp cumin seeds, bashed using a mortar and pestle

125 ml (½ cup) red wine

1 x 400 g (14 oz) tin chopped tomatoes

750 ml (3 cups) beef-style stock

2 bay leaves

500 g (1 lb 2 oz) cauliflower (about 1 large head), stalk and florets finely chopped

375 ml (1½ cups) milk

1–2 tbsp white vinegar or lemon juice

1–2 tbsp soy sauce or tamari

basil leaves, to serve

Polenta

500 ml (2 cups) milk

1 vegetable stock cube

185 g (1¼ cups) polenta

75 g (¾ cup) grated parmesan

I genuinely think that if you served this to someone who didn't know what they were eating, they'd have no idea that cauliflower is the hero in this dish. This ragout transforms the humble vegetable into a super-rich and flavourful stew that is delicious over this silky polenta, but would also be great with pasta, in lasagne, over rice or mashed potatoes. It's a perfect comforting meal on a cooler night, and a great one to make for friends or family because it only develops in flavour, stored happily for days in the fridge. Milk might seem like an odd addition here, but go with it. The hit of creamy, fattiness at the end really adds a certain edge that is sometimes tricky to create in a vegetable-based ragout. Go the extra mile and add a generous drizzle of olive oil or a knob of butter at the end, if you like.

Heat the olive oil, onion and carrot in a large, heavy-based saucepan over medium heat and cook, stirring every couple of minutes, for 10–15 minutes, until the onion is beginning to caramelise and the carrot has sweated out some of its water. Stir through the garlic, then add the tomato paste, stirring it through the vegetables. Reduce the heat a little, and cook, stirring often, for 10 minutes. Add the walnuts, dried herbs and cumin, along with the red wine. As the wine hits the hot pan it'll sizzle and deglaze any sticky tomato bits. Gently scrape the base of the pan with your wooden spoon to remove any stuck-on bits, then add the tomatoes, rinse the tin with a splash of water and add that to the pan as well, along with the beef-style stock and bay leaves. Mix well to combine, then load in all the finely chopped cauliflower, stirring so it's submerged in the liquid. Cover with a lid and leave the ragout to gently simmer for at least 45 minutes over low heat, returning every 10 minutes or so to stir it well. As the cauliflower cooks down it will eventually thicken and become rich and a deep-red colour. If it needs a little more liquid as it cooks, add some water or extra stock.

While the ragout cooks, prepare the polenta by heating the milk, 750 ml (3 cups) of water and the stock cube in a saucepan over medium heat. When the liquid starts to come to the boil, slowly pour in the polenta in a steady stream, whisking as you go to prevent any lumps forming. Reduce the heat to low and let it cook for 20 or so minutes, whisking often to prevent the polenta from sticking or burning. If you're using instant polenta, reduce the cooking time accordingly. Stir through the parmesan until completely melted and check for seasoning.

Add the milk to the ragout and stir to combine. Cook for a further 5 minutes, then finish with the vinegar or lemon juice and soy sauce or tamari to taste. These final ingredients add some welcome salt and tartness, so add a little, mix, then taste and add more until you're happy with the flavour.

Serve the ragout spooned over the soft polenta in individual bowls, or on one big plate in the centre of the table, ready for people to spoon out their own portions as they please. Finish with a few basil leaves scattered over the top. ✳

Swaps

Vegan – milk: plant-based milk; parmesan: vegetable stock cube, nutritional yeast or vegan parmesan

Cauliflower – 750 g–1 kg (1 lb 11 oz–2 lb 3 oz) chopped mushrooms or 2–3 cups cooked lentils or beans

Eggplant

Eggplant (aubergine) is the vegetarian's eternal friend. It makes
a wonderful substitute at a barbecue or in a lasagne and works
well across so many cuisines. Though let's be real – cooked
poorly, eggplant can be rubbery and flavourless. Take the time
to cook them properly, to achieve those silky-soft insides,
and always season your eggplants generously. Most of these
eggplant recipes are quite simple, but I suspect some might
become staples in your cooking repertoire, as they have for me.

With Lachy, Juhi, Alice, Fiona and Frankie

Describe your household

Our house is jam-packed with six people, two chickens and one dog (and one heavy-footed possum). Most of us have known each other for more than 10 years and so living together comes quite easily. We have quite a mixed bag of professions – a physiotherapist, teacher, engineer, public servant, commercial analyst and a technology sales person. We live together happily as one, mostly functional, family.

Do you share food as a household? How often and what does that involve?

We mostly cook our own meals, but there's always somebody scrounging for leftovers. During the lockdown periods, we made a habit of coming together each day to make extravagant meals that we wouldn't be able to achieve alone. Monday's are busy in our kitchen, with most people doing some kind of meal prep to see them through the week.

What's your favourite way to cook/eat eggplant?

Eggplant (aubergine), along with zucchini (courgette), is a staple in most meals. We've recently been getting into Ottolenghi's cookbooks and his recipes often seem to highlight eggplant. A favourite is his steamed eggplant recipe, with a kecap manis, mirin, sesame oil, soy and rice vinegar sauce and heaps of garlic, ginger and chilli, finished with a protein. Easy to make and always tasty!

What does a typical Saturday morning in your house look like?

Saturday mornings in our household usually look like an 8 am meeting in the hall, all bedraggled in our pyjamas, deciding whether we should go to West End Coffee House for breakfast or the markets. Often the markets wins, and we all go and lay on a picnic blanket on the oval with varying breakfasts. Our pup has recently been able to join us at the markets, which makes it another adventure entirely.

What gives you and your housemates hope for a better world?

Living in such a big home has reminded us of the importance of community, and there's a lot of hope in that. Over our many dinners together, we have developed quite the plan for our emerging commune when the world crumbles around us. Tim will build our garden beds and water supply, I will teach the children, Fiona will sew all our clothes, Juhi will fix our sore bodies, Lachy will make sure that we have a telecommunication system and Alice will keep us all on track with her spreadsheets. The chickens will lay us eggs and Tiggy (the dog) will bring the happiness while also being our seccy. *

Afghan-inspired shredded eggplant with mint yoghurt

Serves 4–6 · Gluten Free

3–4 eggplants (aubergines) (about 1.2 kg/2 lb 10 oz)

125 ml (½ cup) olive oil

3 garlic cloves, finely minced

1 tsp ground cumin

1 tsp ground turmeric

1 tsp smoky paprika

¼ tsp cayenne pepper (less if you don't like spice)

1 x 400 g (14 oz) tin crushed tomatoes

salt and pepper

small handful of fresh herbs, to serve

Mint yoghurt

375 g (1½ cups) natural yoghurt

½ bunch of mint, leaves finely chopped

1 tbsp freshly squeezed lemon juice

2 tbsp olive oil

salt and pepper

Swaps

Vegan – yoghurt: coconut yoghurt stirred with a little tahini

This delicious eggplant dish is inspired by borani banjan, a traditional Afghan dish that I never fail to order when eating at my local. In this version of the classic the eggplant is steamed and shredded instead of sliced and deep fried. It's definitely not as mouth-watering as the real deal, but I think it is a really cool way to cook eggplant, creating the same silkiness you get from broiling, but less messy and more hands-off. The cool, minty yoghurt finishes this dish so deliciously, I challenge you not to lick the plate clean.

Prepare a steamer and set over medium heat. Add the eggplants (halve them if you need to), then cover with a tight-fitting lid and steam for 25–30 minutes, until the eggplants are completely soft. Remove from the heat and leave the lid on, allowing them to continue steaming while you prepare the other elements. If you don't have a steamer, you can DIY this step by using a colander or by placing a heatproof plate on top of rolled-up balls of foil in the base of a pan with the boiling water. Alternatively, roast the whole eggplants in a preheated 220°C (430°F) fan-forced oven for 40–50 minutes, until they're cooked all the way through.

While the eggplants cook, heat the olive oil in a large frying pan over low heat. Add the garlic and cook gently for a few minutes, stirring often. Add the spices and cook for another minute, then add the crushed tomatoes. Rinse the tin with a little water and add that in too. Season the sauce well with salt and pepper (the eggplant is unseasoned, so the sauce should taste quite salty – add at least two big pinches of salt). Bring the sauce to a slow simmer and cook for 5–10 minutes, until reduced to a thick and dark-red sauce. Turn off the heat.

Meanwhile, mix together all the ingredients for the mint yoghurt and 2 tablespoons of water in a small bowl. Season with a pinch of salt and pepper.

Carefully remove the steamed eggplants and peel and discard the skin. Tear each eggplant into three or four chunky pieces, or scoop out the flesh with a spoon. Add the shredded eggplant to the tomato sauce and stir really well to coat everything and break down the eggplant further. Return the pan to medium heat and allow the eggplant to cook in the sauce for 5–10 minutes. Taste a piece and add more seasoning if needed.

Transfer the eggplant and tomato to a serving dish, then pour or scoop the yoghurt sauce over the top and scatter across the herbs. Serve the dish warm or close to room temperature, with steamed rice and some flatbread, and a simple chopped cucumber and tomato salad.

This dish keeps wonderfully for leftovers. The flavours continue to develop in the fridge, making this a great meal to make ahead. ✳

Eggplant parma sandwiches

Makes 4

1 large or 2 small eggplants (aubergines), sliced lengthways into at least four 1.5 cm (½ in) thick 'steaks'

80 ml (⅓ cup) olive oil, plus extra for drizzling (optional)

salt and pepper

1 egg

80 ml (⅓ cup) milk

75 g (½ cup) plain (all-purpose) flour

1 tsp smoky paprika

1 tsp dried oregano

1 tsp garlic powder

120 g (2 cups) panko breadcrumbs (or homemade breadcrumbs)

200 g (7 oz) fresh mozzarella, thinly sliced

50 g (½ cup) grated parmesan

Simple tomato sauce

60 ml (¼ cup) olive oil

3 garlic cloves, thinly sliced

½ tsp dried basil

½ tsp dried oregano

2 tbsp tomato paste (concentrated purée)

2 x 400 g (14 oz) tins crushed tomatoes

To serve

1 baguette, divided into four, or 4 panini rolls, sliced open

2 tbsp salted butter

handful of basil leaves

I serve these parmas on fresh baguettes here, but they're equally delicious on their own with some salad or soft polenta as a great main-meal alternative that I defer to often. Unlike most crumbed eggplant that you might see as the single vegetarian offering at the country-town pub, these slabs are oven-baked and avoid being overly rich and oily. They also avoid the undercooked rubbery eggplant trap by spending three lots of time in the oven, ensuring that each final piece is crunchy and golden on the outside, but silky and soft on the inside. As you cut your raw eggplant, it's a good idea to remove some of the skin from the outer slices, as the breadcrumb mixture doesn't stick as well to it. If you have leftover tomato pasta sauce, or a jar of quality pre-made sauce to use up, feel free to sub that in for the homemade sauce here to make things even easier.

Preheat the oven to 180°C (350°F). Line a large baking tray with baking paper.

Lay the eggplant slices on the prepared tray and drizzle over half the olive oil. Sprinkle each piece with a pinch of salt and pepper, then transfer to the oven and bake for 10–15 minutes, until just turning golden and starting to soften. Remove from the oven and leave to cool for 5 minutes.

Meanwhile, prepare a crumbing station. Whisk the egg and milk in one shallow bowl, combine the flour, 1 tsp of salt, the paprika, oregano and garlic powder in another bowl and place the breadcrumbs in a third bowl.

Once cool enough to handle, coat each piece of eggplant thoroughly in the seasoned flour, then carefully dunk in the egg wash, until completely coated. Finally, transfer to the breadcrumbs and press the crumbs firmly on both sides until the eggplant is covered. Place the crumbed eggplant on the baking tray, drizzle over the remaining olive oil and sprinkle with salt and pepper, then return the tray to the oven and cook for 30 minutes, flipping the eggplant halfway through cooking until golden and crisp on the outside and soft inside.

As the crumbed eggplant cooks, prepare the tomato sauce by heating the olive oil in a saucepan over medium heat. Add the garlic and dried herbs and stir well for about 1 minute, until the garlic is fragrant. Add the tomato paste and cook for 1–2 minutes, stirring frequently, then add the crushed tomatoes, rinse out the tomato tins with a splash of water and add this to the pan too. Season the sauce with salt and pepper, then reduce the heat to low and cook, stirring frequently, for 10–15 minutes, until reduced.

Remove the eggplant from the oven and spoon a generous amount of the sauce over each slice. Arrange the mozzarella over the top, then sprinkle over the parmesan. Return the eggplant to the oven for a further 5–8 minutes, until the mozzarella has melted and the parmesan is lightly golden. Warm your baguettes or rolls in the oven during the last 2 minutes of cooking.

Assemble the sandwiches by buttering the warm bread. Top with the crumbed saucy eggplant, a few basil leaves and an extra drizzle of olive oil, if you like. ✳

Swaps

Gluten free – breadcrumbs: polenta; baguette: gluten-free bread or serve over cooked polenta

Vegan – egg wash: 250 ml (1 cup) plant-based milk; mozzarella and parmesan: vegan cheese; butter: olive oil

Eggplants (aubergines) – mushrooms or zucchini (courgettes)

Potato rosti with baba ghanoush & pomegranate salsa

Serves 4–5 · Vegan · Gluten Free

6 large potatoes (about 1.2 kg/2 lb 10 oz), scrubbed

125 ml (½ cup) vegetable oil

1 heaped tsp flaky salt

Baba ghanoush

2 eggplants (aubergines) (about 1 kg/2 lb 3 oz)

125 ml (½ cup) olive oil

½ tsp salt

65 g (¼ cup) tahini

1 tbsp freshly squeezed lemon juice, plus extra if needed

2 garlic cloves, peeled

60 ml (¼ cup) cold water

Pomegranate salsa

1 pomegranate, seeds removed

½ bunch of mint, leaves shredded

2 large tomatoes, finely diced

¼ red onion, finely diced

1 tbsp pomegranate molasses

1 tbsp olive oil

1 tbsp freshly squeezed lemon juice, plus extra if needed

salt and pepper

Swaps

Pomegranate – 200 g (1 cup) diced tomatoes plus some dried currants or cranberries if you have them

Pomegranate molasses – 1:1 ratio of balsamic vinegar and maple syrup, or raspberry jam or cranberry sauce

These beautifully topped rostis make a special breakfast, lunch or dinner. They're punchy in flavour and texture, and look just lovely too. Sometimes I make miniature versions as a classy little canape. A tip for deseeding your pomegranate: quarter it, then submerge in a bowl of water and use your hands to pop out all the seeds. The white pith will rise to the top, making it easy to discard.

Place the potatoes in a large saucepan and cover with cold water. Sprinkle in a generous pinch of salt, then bring to the boil over medium heat and cook for 10 minutes or until a fork can just stab through them, with a lot of resistance. When parboiling the potatoes, take care not to overcook them; this will ensure a crispier rosti. Drain the potatoes and set aside to cool completely. This step can be done up to 2 days ahead.

Once the potatoes have cooled, preheat the oven to 200°C (400°F) fan-forced. Line a large baking tray with baking paper.

Grate the potatoes using the largest holes on a box grater, then transfer to a bowl, along with the olive oil and salt and mix well to combine. Taste the mixture and ensure there's enough salt. Press the grated potato mix into 8–10 balls, squishing it with your hands so that the potato is as tightly packed as possible, then press down to flatten a little. Bake for about 40 minutes, flipping halfway through cooking, until the rosti are golden and crispy.

Meanwhile, to make the baba ghanoush, cook the eggplants either directly over a gas flame, turning with tongs every couple of minutes for 15–20 minutes, or on a barbecue grill plate, preheated to high, with the lid closed. If neither is an option you can also slice the eggplant in half and lay them, flesh-side down, on a lined baking tray and cook in the oven for 40–50 minutes, until collapsed. To ensure you really get that smoky flavour, cook the eggplant until they're really black on the outside and completely soft on the inside.

Prepare the pomegranate salsa by combining everything in a bowl and seasoning well. Taste and adjust the seasoning and lemon juice as needed.

Once the eggplant is ready, carefully remove and discard the skin, then transfer the flesh to a food processor or a jug with a stick blender. Add the remaining baba ghanoush ingredients except the cold water. Blend the mixture until thick and smooth, then, with the motor running on low speed, slowly pour in the water. Taste the mixture and add more salt or lemon as needed. If you don't have a food processor, just grate the garlic and mash the eggplant flesh well with a fork before stirring everything together in a bowl.

Assemble the rosti by serving two to a plate, topped with a generous few tablespoons of baba ghanoush and a serving of the pomegranate salsa. ✳

Slow-cooked eggplant caponata

Serves 4–6 as a main, or 8–10 as a side · Vegan · Gluten Free

80 ml (⅓ cup) olive oil, plus extra for drizzling

80 g (½ cup) pine nuts

4 spring onions (scallions), thinly sliced

3 celery stalks, finely diced

60 g (½ cup) sultanas (golden raisins)

2 tbsp capers, rinsed and drained

1 tsp smoky paprika

2 tbsp brown sugar, plus extra if needed

2 eggplants (aubergines), cut into 1–2 cm (½–¾ in) cubes

salt and pepper

2 x 400 g (14 oz) cans chopped tomatoes

2 tbsp red wine vinegar

½ bunch of mint, leaves picked, plus extra to serve

Caponata is a Sicilian dish that I fell in love with at first bite. It's such a perfect balance of sweet, salty and tart. This one-pot wonder version is absolutely packed with flavour, and is much less of a fuss to make than most caponata recipes, as there's no need to pre-cook the eggplant. The flavours really develop in the hour or two that it's left to simmer over low heat, so plan ahead and ensure that you give it enough time. I love serving this dish as the centrepiece of an Italian spread, but it's also delightful with pasta, over soft polenta or simply alongside some roast potatoes and salad. It will keep wonderfully for days, and is great hot, cold or at room temperature.

Heat the olive oil in a large, heavy-based saucepan or frying pan over medium heat. Add the pine nuts and cook, stirring frequently, for 2 minutes or until they're just beginning to brown and the oil has begun to foam a little (watch them closely to ensure they don't burn). Carefully scoop out half the nuts, setting them aside in a bowl. Add the spring onion and celery to the pan, then reduce the heat to low and cook for about 5 minutes, until the veggies are starting to turn translucent. Add the sultanas, capers, paprika and sugar and stir well to combine.

Increase the heat a little and add the eggplant, along with an extra drizzle of olive oil, a pinch of salt and pepper and 60–80 ml (¼–⅓ cup) of water. Stir well to coat the eggplant in the mixture, then cook for 5–10 minutes, until the eggplant has softened. Add the tomatoes, rinse each tin with a splash of water and add that in too. Stir the caponata well and allow it to come to a slow simmer before reducing the heat to as low as your stovetop will go. Cover the pan with a lid and leave it to slowly bubble away for 1–2 hours, returning to stir it every 15 or so minutes, to ensure that the caponata doesn't stick to the base of the pan.

Once the caponata looks silky and rich, taste and adjust the seasoning to your liking, adding a little more sugar if it's quite tart. Stir through the vinegar and mint leaves.

Serve with the reserved pine nuts scattered over the top, along with a few extra mint leaves. ✳

A big moussaka

Serves 6–8

3 large eggplants (aubergines), cut lengthways into 2–3 mm (⅛ in) thick slices

3 large potatoes, cut lengthways into 1–2 mm (¹⁄₁₆–⅛ in) thick slices

60 ml (¼ cup) olive oil, plus extra for drizzling

salt and pepper

1 large onion, finely diced

1 large carrot, finely diced

3 celery stalks, finely diced

20 g (¾ oz) dried mushrooms (porcini are ideal, but shiitake or another dried mushroom will be fine)

500 ml (2 cups) boiling water

5 garlic cloves, minced

3 tbsp currants

1 tsp ground cinnamon

1 tsp ground cumin

1 tsp ground coriander

120 g (1½ cups) TVP mince (or 300 g/10½ oz fresh plant-based mince)

750 g (3 cups) tomato passata (puréed tomatoes)

250 ml (1 cup) vegetable stock

White sauce

60 g (2 oz) salted butter

75 g (½ cup) plain (all-purpose) flour

625 ml (2½ cups) milk

pinch of nutmeg (ideally freshly grated)

salt and pepper

The first time I made moussaka I was about 12 years old, and I distinctly remember mis-reading 1 teaspoon of cinnamon for 1 tablespoon and ending up with a very strange, cinnamon-y meal that turned me off this dish for a long time. But it's so bloody delicious! Here's a vegetarian version of the traditionally lamb-based Greek signature made using a beautifully flavoursome fake-meat ragout. It's a bit of work, but this delicious bake will feed the masses and makes incredible leftovers. It's a nice recipe to add to your group meals repertoire if you've already nailed lasagne. Adjust the filling as you like, adding in any extra veggies you might have on hand that need using up.

Preheat the oven to 200°C (400°F) fan-forced. Line two large baking trays with baking paper.

Arrange the eggplant and potato slices across both trays (don't worry if a few are overlapping), drizzle with a little olive oil and season with salt and pepper. Transfer to the oven and cook for 25–35 minutes, turning the veggies over halfway through cooking. Sometimes I cook the vegetables in my sandwich press instead, which works equally well and delays heating up the kitchen so much.

Meanwhile, heat the olive oil in a large, heavy-based saucepan over medium heat. Add the onion, carrot and celery and cook, stirring often, for 15–20 minutes, until reduced and golden.

While the veggies cook, rehydrate the dried mushrooms in the boiling water in a small bowl. Cover and set aside for 10 minutes. Remove the mushrooms from the water and chop them finely, reserving the soaking liquid. Add the mushroom to the pan and cook for another couple of minutes, then add the garlic, currants and spices. Mix well and cook for 2 minutes or until fragrant, then stir in the TVP mince, followed by the passata, vegetable stock and reserved mushroom soaking liquid, along with a little salt and pepper. Stir well, then reduce the heat to low and cook for at least 20 minutes, or up to an hour, adding a little more water if it reduces too much, until the mixture is thick and luscious.

As the filling cooks, prepare the white sauce by melting the butter in a saucepan over medium heat until bubbling. Add the flour and whisk well for a couple of minutes to form a thick paste. Slowly pour in the milk as you continue to whisk, then add the nutmeg and some salt and pepper and keep whisking for about 2 minutes until the sauce thickens. Remove from the heat, check the seasoning and adjust as needed, then set aside.

To assemble

200 g (7 oz) dried lasagne sheets

70 g (⅔ cup) grated cheese (cheddar or a mixture of whatever you have on hand)

60 g (1 cup) panko breadcrumbs

small handful of flat-leaf parsley leaves, to serve (optional)

Swaps

Vegan – butter: vegan margarine; milk: plant-based milk; omit the cheese

Gluten free – lasagne sheets: gluten-free pasta sheets; plain (all-purpose) flour: cornflour (corn starch) or gluten-free plain flour

Dried mushrooms – 200 g (7 oz) fresh mushrooms plus 500 ml (2 cups) vegetable stock

TVP – 2 x 400 g (14 oz) tins drained lentils or a mixture of lentils and cooked mushrooms

To assemble the moussaka, spread a tablespoon of the 'mince' sauce in the base of a 30 x 20 cm (12 x 8 in) baking dish. Add a layer of lasagne sheets, then spoon over a generous layer of 'mince' (reserving at least half). Add half the eggplant slices, then half the roasted potato slices. Drizzle over one-third of the white sauce. Top with another layer of lasagne sheets and repeat the layering, finishing with a final layer of white sauce. Scatter over the cheese and breadcrumbs, then transfer to the oven and bake for 30–40 minutes at 180°C (350°F), until the top is browning and the lasagne sheets are just tender when stabbed with a fork. Allow the dish to stand for 15 minutes before serving so it's easier to cut. Scatter with parsley leaves (if using) and dig in.

Store the leftovers in an airtight container in the fridge for 3–4 days. ✳

Kale

It's funny to think that 10 years ago kale really wasn't a common vegetable at all. Rumour has it that before 2012, Pizza Hut was the largest buyer of the stuff, where it was used as garnish in their cabinets. Hilarious. Now, it's a staple in many kitchens and gardens and my go-to leafy green, partly because of its long fridge life but also its ability to retain some good substance in a dish, unlike spinach or other leafies. If you're eating kale raw, take a minute to massage the leaves first with a bit of olive oil and lemon juice, plus seasoning. Rubbing these ingredients into the leaves helps to tenderise them and take out some of the toughness. These recipes use a mixture of curly kale and cavolo nero (also known as Tuscan kale or black cabbage). The latter is generally my preference, but can be tricky to find, so you can use them interchangeably if you need to.

With Liz, Rhett, Meg and Jamie

Describe your household

Two couples (Meg and Jamie; Liz and Rhett) living under the tyrannical rule of one annoying cat, Eno.

Who's the best cook in your house and why?

We're a very self-confident household and we each voted for ourselves: Meg thinks she's the best because she's inconsistent but unexpectedly unexpected; Jamie voted for himself because he's efficient and can pull something together with very few ingredients; Rhett thinks he's the most accurate with executing recipes — indeed he is the only one who follows recipes, and he bakes; and Liz backs herself because she's from fancy Adelaide and was spoon-fed on tapenade and varietals.

What does a typical Saturday morning in your house look like?

Our first call of the day is 3.30 am, when Eno wakes and starts clawing Rhett's face and meowing at Jamie and Meg's bedroom door. After gently drifting back to sleep, the sound of leaf blowers fires up and the suburban symphony begins. Then we complain about it on the text thread for an hour or so before rising for breakfast.

What do you love about living in a share house generally, or about this house in particular?

Before we moved in together, we were living separately. So we each made the call to return to share-housing in our thirties/forties and do it right. It's way better now that we have careers and access to therapy.

How do you navigate sharing a kitchen?

We have a two-fridge system, but otherwise everything is pooled. We mainly cook separately and only make food for each other when everyone's up for it. ✳

Greens pizza

Serves 4–6

1 scant tsp instant dried yeast

375 ml (1½ cups) lukewarm water

1 tbsp honey or sugar

2 tbsp olive oil

2 scant tsp salt

450 g (3 cups) plain (all-purpose) or 00 flour, plus extra for dusting

Topping

bunch of basil, leaves picked

small handful of oregano leaves

4–5 spring onions (scallions), thinly sliced

2 tbsp olive oil, plus extra for drizzling

zest and juice of 1 small lemon

250 ml (1 cup) double-thickened (dollop) cream

50 g (½ cup) grated parmesan

1 tbsp white wine vinegar

½ tsp white pepper

salt

large bunch of cavolo nero, leaves stripped and torn into large pieces

300 g (10½ oz) fresh mozzarella, sliced

Swaps

Vegan – cream: vegan aioli, cashew cream or vegan sour cream; parmesan: 40 g (⅔ cup) nutritional yeast; mozzarella: roasted eggplant

A bubbly, chewy pizza base topped with a mega luscious and flavourful herby cream and crunchy kale is a perfect way to end the day. You could top it with more ingredients (olives, pine nuts, broccolini or fresh mint would all be delightful additions), or switch the kale for mushrooms, roasted eggplant or thin slices of potato. I must say though, there's something about the simplicity of this pizza that is really lovely. The real hero is the generous slathering of the creamy herb sauce, which in my opinion trumps other non-tomato pizza alternatives. If you're organised enough, I recommend making the pizza dough a day ahead; the extra day in the fridge really improves the consistency and flavour.

In a large mixing bowl, whisk together the yeast, warm water and honey, then leave to stand for 10 minutes or until foamy. Add the olive oil, salt and flour, whisking with a fork until a shaggy dough forms. Dust your hands lightly in flour, then fold the dough over itself a few times in the bowl, to shape it into a ball. It's a very wet and sticky dough, which helps make a better, chewier pizza, so don't fret if it's sticking to your hands a bit (you don't need to knead it). Once you have folded it over a number of times, scrape any dough from your hands, then give them a wash.

Cover the bowl with a damp tea towel and put it in a warm spot. Leave it to rise for 1 hour, then, using wet hands, gently stretch and fold the dough onto itself a few times. Cover again and leave for another 30–60 minutes, until doubled in size. Alternatively, you can pop the covered bowl in the fridge and leave the dough to rise slowly for 12–24 hours, which I definitely recommend for optimal dough.

Scrape the dough onto a floured work surface, knocking out the air in the process. Divide the dough into four pieces, or however many pizzas you'd like to make, and give each piece a little sprinkle of flour. Leave the dough for 5 minutes to relax the glutens, which makes the dough easier to shape. Transfer the dough to four large squares of baking paper, then use your hands to pull and stretch each piece into a rough 20 cm (8 in) circle, leaving the outer lip a little less stretched if you like a more substantial crust (picking it up and gently shaking it to stretch helps get it nice and thin in the middle). Leave the dough to prove while you preheat the oven to its hottest temperature – usually around 250°C (480°F) fan-forced.

To make the topping, bash the basil, oregano, two of the sliced spring onions, the olive oil and lemon zest together using a mortar and pestle to form a rough paste. If you don't have a mortar and pestle, simply chop the ingredients together on a large board or whiz them in a food processor with a little water, which will give you a more vibrant green sauce, as I have done here. Combine the paste with the cream, parmesan, white wine vinegar, white pepper and a generous pinch of salt to taste. Stir the mixture until combined. →

In a separate bowl or on a board, drizzle a little olive oil over the cavolo nero and add the lemon juice, along with a pinch of salt. Gently massage the leaves to tenderise them and infuse the flavour.

Once the oven is close to temperature, spread a generous few tablespoons of the creamy green sauce onto each pizza base. Transfer the pizza bases to baking trays and cook for 8–10 minutes, until the sauce is bubbling and the crust has puffed up and is beginning to brown. Remove the pizzas from the oven and scatter over the cavolo nero (which will shrink substantially when cooked), the mozzarella and remaining spring onion. Return to the oven for a final 3–4 minutes, until the kale is wilted and beginning to crisp and the crust is golden.

Transfer the pizzas to a chopping board and slice up. Serve with an extra drizzle of olive oil and a pinch of flaky salt, if you like. ✳

My go-to kale salad

Serves 6–8 as a side · Vegan · Gluten Free

60 ml (¼ cup) olive oil

100 g (¾ cup) pumpkin seeds (pepitas)

50 g (⅓ cup) currants

salt and pepper

1 tbsp honey or maple syrup

large bunch of kale, leaves stripped and finely shredded

juice of 1 lemon (about 2 tbsp)

½ red onion, finely diced

1 avocado, finely diced

2–3 large tomatoes, finely diced

Swaps

Tomatoes or avocado – cucumber, sautéed mushrooms, capsicum (bell pepper), sweetcorn or other veggies you have on hand

The first time I made this salad I was on a camping trip with my three oldest friends on Quandamooka Country at Minjerribah. We'd found ourselves with an odd collection of ingredients at the end of a week's holiday that I threw together to go alongside our regular lunch of an unholy portion of hot chips. It's been a go-to since then, and is delightfully flexible. I've kept it very basic here, with avocado and tomato because they are always on my pantry shelf, but you could throw in diced cucumbers, leftover roasted vegetables, herbs or cheese, such as feta or haloumi. The salad itself is only lightly dressed, but the pops of salty sweet from the pumpkin seeds and currants flavour the whole thing perfectly.

Warm half the olive oil in a frying pan over medium heat. Add the pumpkin seeds and currants and cook, stirring often, for 3–4 minutes, until the pumpkin seeds start to pop and turn golden. Season well with salt and pepper, then drizzle over the honey or maple syrup – it should sizzle and bubble. Transfer the mixture to a bowl or your chopping board to cool a little. Wash your pan in warm water right away, or it'll be a pain to clean later.

Combine the kale with the remaining olive oil, the lemon juice and a good sprinkle of salt and pepper in a serving bowl. Use your hands to massage the kale, rubbing the seasonings into the leaves. The kale will turn a little darker and become glossy.

Add most of the pumpkin seed mixture, the onion, avocado and tomato, along with any other ingredients you're adding, and toss well to combine. Sprinkle the remaining pumpkin seed mixture over the top and serve. ✳

Creamy cavolo nero, risoni & mushroom bake

Serves 4–6

bunch of cavolo nero, leaves picked and roughly shredded

bunch of basil, leaves picked, plus extra to serve

4 garlic cloves, peeled

250 ml (1 cup) pouring cream

salt and pepper

juice of 1 lemon (about 2 tbsp)

750 ml–1 litre (3–4 cups) vegetable stock

500 g (1 lb 2 oz) risoni

300 g (10½ oz) button mushrooms, thinly sliced

2 tbsp olive oil, plus extra for drizzling

100 g (1 cup) grated parmesan

250 g (9 oz) burrata, plus 125 ml (½ cup) of its soaking liquid (whey)

lemon wedges, to serve

Swaps

Gluten free – risoni: small gluten-free pasta, quinoa or rice

Vegan – cream: plant-based milk or oat cream; parmesan: nutritional yeast; omit the burrata and top the bake with slow-roasted tomatoes, potatoes, eggplant (aubergine) or caramelised onion

Burrata whey – 125 ml (½ cup) milk or extra cream

Cavolo nero – curly kale, silverbeet (Swiss chard) or spinach

Mushrooms – tomatoes, zucchini (courgettes), brussels sprouts, eggplant or marinated artichokes

This pasta-bake-esque meal is perfect for something special on a busy night as it basically only involves two steps: first, make the sauce and combine it with everything else; second, bake the whole dish until the risoni is cooked through. The result is a vibrant green, vaguely pesto-scented creamy bake with pockets of creamy burrata and golden mushrooms that's very moreish and satisfying. If you can't find cavolo nero (also known as Tuscan kale), curly kale is absolutely fine too – the colour just might be a little more subtle. I use the soaking whey from the burrata here as a final liquid addition to help finish cooking the risoni. If you aren't already cooking with your whey, it's basically just seasoned water, so it's good to sneak into all sorts of recipes that call for stock, milk or water.

Preheat the oven to 220°C (430°F) fan-forced.

Place the cavolo nero, basil, garlic and three-quarters of the cream in a high powered blender and blitz to a green purée. Generously season with salt and pepper. Depending on the size and power of your blender you might need to do this in two batches.

Pour the mixture into a 30 x 20 cm (12 x 8 in) baking dish (or a 25 cm/10 in round dish), add the lemon juice and 750 ml (3 cups) of the stock and gently whisk to combine. Tip in the risoni and gently mix to spread the pasta evenly through the liquid. Scatter the mushroom on top, spreading them as much as you can, but not mixing them into the liquid. Drizzle over the olive oil and sprinkle with some salt and pepper.

Transfer the dish to the oven and bake for 20 minutes, until the mushroom is deep golden brown and the dish is bubbling. Remove the dish from the oven, scatter over the parmesan, then gently stir the mushrooms and cheese through the risoni. Add the burrata whey and stir it through to combine. At this point taste the mixture and adjust the seasoning if necessary. If the risoni is still undercooked and the liquid has evaporated, add the remaining stock.

Return the bake to the oven for a final 5–10 minutes, until the pasta is just cooked. Tear up the burrata and place it evenly over the pasta bake, nestling some pieces in the risoni. Right before serving, spoon over the reserved cream, scatter with a few basil leaves and drizzle with a little extra olive oil. Serve with lemon wedges. ✳

Kale & chipotle tofu bowls

Serves 4–6 · Vegan · Gluten Free

large bunch of kale (any variety), leaves stripped and roughly chopped

2 tbsp olive oil

1 tbsp red wine vinegar

salt and pepper

300–450 g (2–3 cups) cooked rice or other grains

1–2 carrots, grated

4–5 radishes, thinly sliced

80 g (2¾ oz) pickles or kraut

Chipotle tofu

350 g (12½ oz) firm tofu

60 ml (¼ cup) chipotle sauce

1 tsp liquid smoke

2 tsp red wine vinegar

1 tsp stock powder (or ½ stock cube)

150 g (1 cup) plain (all-purpose) flour

1 heaped tsp ground cumin

1 heaped tsp smoky paprika

½ tsp salt

olive oil, for drizzling

Zesty green sauce

½ large bunch of coriander (cilantro) stems and leaves

30 g (1 oz) pickled jalapenos

1 avocado, flesh scooped out

2 tbsp olive oil

2 tbsp freshly squeezed lime juice

salt and pepper

This is what you should cook for dinner when you have that post-too-many-bowls-of-hot-chips or other salty/sugary foods feeling ('junk mouth', as my sister Elly calls it). This is more of an idea than a recipe, because as long as you have a hearty base, an unholy amount of fresh greens, a very generously flavoured sauce, some smoky baked tofu and extra veggies or pickles for crunch, you'll have yourself a good and satisfying meal. This recipe is one of my go-to versions, but substitute and swap the toppings to use up whatever you have. Extra fresh herbs, toasted nuts, feta or haloumi and roasted vegetables all make excellent additions.

To make the chipotle tofu, slice the tofu into 2 cm (¾ in) thick slabs, then wrap in a paper towel or a clean tea towel and place a heavy chopping board on top. Leave the tofu to drain for 10 minutes, then slice into cubes. Combine the chipotle sauce, liquid smoke, red wine vinegar and stock powder in a bowl then add the tofu and gently toss to coat. Set aside to marinate for 20 minutes, or place in the fridge for up to 24 hours.

Preheat the oven to 200°C (400°F) fan-forced.

Combine the flour, cumin, paprika and salt in a bowl. Coat each piece of tofu in the flour mixture, then spread them evenly across a large baking tray. Drizzle with a little olive oil and bake for 25–30 minutes, turning over halfway through cooking, until the tofu has formed a crust and is a little darker in colour.

Blitz everything for the zesty green sauce in a blender until smooth. Taste and season generously with salt and pepper.

Place the kale in a large bowl and add the olive oil, red wine vinegar and a generous sprinkle of salt and pepper. Massage the leaves with your hands for about 30 seconds to tenderise them.

Divide the rice or other grains among bowls, then add the kale, tofu, carrot, radish and pickles or kraut in portions. Scoop the sauce into the middle of each bowl for dipping, or swirl it through, and serve. ✳

Kale dal

Serves 8–10 · Vegan · Gluten Free

60 ml (¼ cup) olive oil

1 large onion, finely diced

6 garlic cloves, minced

40 g (1½ oz) ginger, peeled and grated
or finely chopped

375 g (1½ cups) brown lentils,
picked over and rinsed

750 ml–1 litre (3–4 cups) vegetable
stock or water

large bunch of kale, leaves picked and
shredded

1 long green chilli, finely chopped
(optional), plus extra, sliced, to serve

½ bunch of coriander (cilantro) stems
and leaves

150 g (1 cup) raw cashew nuts, soaked
in 250–500 ml (1–2 cups) boiling
water for 20 minutes

1 x 400 ml (13½ fl oz) tin coconut milk

1–2 tsp sugar

juice of 1–2 limes (2–3 tbsp)

Spice mix

1 tbsp cumin seeds

1 tbsp coriander seeds

1 tsp mustard seeds

1 tsp fennel seeds

4–5 cardamom pods

1 tsp ground cinnamon

1 tsp salt

Swaps

*Kale – spinach, silverbeet (Swiss chard)
or mustard leaves*

This recipe replaces the traditional spinach and mustard greens used in saag for kale, to make a sort-of-saag dal. It's a bit more involved than the dal you might make regularly, but it's worth it for the rich and beautiful taste. Blended soaked cashews and coconut milk make for a good whack of creaminess and a silky texture. This recipe makes a lot of dal, because it holds incredibly well for days and the flavours only get better with time. If you end up with too much, it's a perfect Tupperware meal to drop round to a friend or neighbour.

Heat a large heavy-based saucepan or deep frying pan over medium heat and add all the spice mix ingredients. Cook, tossing frequently, for 2–3 minutes, until fragrant and beginning to pop. Pour the spices into a mortar and (or a bowl) and set aside to cool.

Next, add the olive oil and diced onion to the warm pan and cook for 10–15 minutes over low heat, until the onion begins to caramelise. Add the garlic and ginger and cook for a further 3–5 minutes, until fragrant.

Meanwhile, grind the spices using the mortar and pestle to a rough powder or pulse them in a food processor.

Add the spices to the pan and stir well to combine. Add the lentils and 750 ml (3 cups) of the stock or water and increase the heat to medium. Bring the mixture to a slow simmer, then reduce the heat back to low and allow the lentils to cook away for 15–20 minutes, adding a little more stock or water if needed.

Blanch the kale in boiling water for 30 seconds maximum, until it brightens in colour, then drain in a colander and run under cold water. It's important not to overcook the kale here, to ensure it retains a beautiful bright-green colour. Add the cooled kale to a high-powered blender, along with the green chilli (if using) and coriander, then drain the cashew nuts and add them too. Blend the mixture until smooth and silky, adding a splash of water if necessary to get the ingredients moving. If you only have a food processor, the kale probably won't break down completely and give you a smooth, creamy texture, but it will still be delicious.

Once the lentils are almost tender, but still have a little bite, add the coconut milk and stir well to combine. Cook for 3–4 minutes, then stir through the kale mixture and turn off the heat, allowing the heat of the lentils to warm it through without losing its vibrant colour. Add 1 teaspoon of the sugar and 2 tablespoons of the lime juice and stir well. Taste the dal and add more sugar, lime juice or salt to taste.

I like to serve the dal with rice, with a splash of green chilli chutney or some sliced green chilli, a swirl of coconut yoghurt and some fresh tomato and cucumber. ✻

Curried egg
& crispy kale ciabattas

Serves 4

8 eggs

125 g (½ cup) whole-egg mayonnaise
(I use Kewpie)

1 tbsp curry powder

60 ml (¼ cup) olive oil

salt and pepper

bunch of kale, leaves stripped and
shredded (about 5 cups)

2–3 tsp Tabasco or other vinegar-
based chilli sauce, to taste

4 ciabatta rolls, or 8 pieces of white
sandwich bread

butter, for spreading

4 dill pickles, thinly sliced

I still remember the first time I tasted curried egg – I was working back of house in a kitchen and would often spend the first blissful hour of the day quietly making sandwich after sandwich to fill the cabinet. My favourite breakfast was the bread crusts loaded with the curried egg mix that I'd munch on as I went. Combined here with tiny pieces of kale so well roasted that they shatter immediately when munched on, this sandwich is delicious in its simple but punchy flavours, and the texture is really addictive. Once you get hooked on kale cooked this way, you'll find it's a texture that's awesome in lots of dishes. If you don't like your eggs with any soft yolks, increase the cooking time, but I do think some squidgy yolk is essential to ensure there's enough moisture in the sandwich. As are soft bread rolls, or even just plain old white sandwich loaf.

Preheat the oven to 200°C (400°F) fan-forced.

Bring a small saucepan of salted water to the boil. Once rapidly boiling, gently lower in the eggs and set a timer for 6 minutes. When the timer goes off, drain the eggs and transfer to a bowl of cold water to halt the cooking process. Alternatively, run under cold running water until the eggs are room temperature.

Meanwhile, combine the mayonnaise, curry powder, 1 tablespoon of the olive oil and a scant pinch of salt and pepper in a bowl and stir well.

Place the kale in a bowl and add the remaining olive oil, a pinch of salt and the Tabasco. Rub the leaves until well coated and shiny, then spread over a large baking tray in an even layer and bake for 10–20 minutes, tossing the leaves halfway through cooking, until crisp and golden. Watch carefully as the leaves can burn quickly, although a few burnt pieces are fine. In the final 2 minutes of cooking, add the ciabatta rolls to warm them through (skip this step if using sandwich bread).

Peel the eggs and roughly slice them into the mayonnaise mixture. Gently stir to coat the egg.

Cut the rolls in half, then butter both sides and divide the curried egg over the bottom half of each roll. Top with a generous handful of kale and finish with the pickles. *

Lemon

Lemons are such a powerhouse, helping so many dishes shine with their incredible aroma, acidity and flavour. When they're in season, I buy them (or source them from friends' fruiting trees) in bulk and zest and juice a heap, freezing the juice in tablespoon quantities in ice-cube trays. While lemons are almost always used as a helping hand to elevate other ingredients, these recipes put them at the centre, where you can really taste their awesome flavour. I'm particularly into the savoury recipes in this chapter, where lemon is used as forwardly as you might expect in a cake or tart.

With Makeda and Harriet

Describe your household

We are Harriet, Makeda and Hildegard (the cat). We live in a little apartment in West End, and we like to play videogames, go to the local pool, take care of our plants and pamper Hildie.

Do you share food as a household? How often and what does that involve?

Harriet is a shift worker so we have conflicting schedules, meaning that we don't get to share meals often. When we do eat together we like to have a dumpling feast and love Laoganma black bean chilli sauce on everything. The Nutribullet is on high rotation making banana, blueberry and spinach smoothies every morning for brekky. Sometimes we'll pop out for a cheeky Indian takeaway and a night-time stroll around West End. Sadly, Hildie has recently been put on a diet, but she previously enjoyed kangaroo mince of an evening.

What's your favourite way to cook/eat lemons?

Harriet inherited a lemon, yoghurt and olive oil cake recipe from her mother, Debbie, which is a family favourite. It can be topped with preserved lemon but does just fine with half a cup of freshly squeezed lemon juice, a whole zested lemon and some icing sugar on top. It's not too sweet and lovely with a cup of tea. If you're a real yoghurt fiend (like Harriet's mum), you can add fresh yoghurt to the side. Makeda puts lemon in everything, and thinks it adds an especially nice twist to baked beans. We have to regularly clean our kitchen benchtop with lemon too, it gets stained with everything!

What does a typical Saturday morning in your house look like?

Either early starts or big sleep-ins (although always big sleep-ins for Hildie). If we're home, a quiet sit on the deck or a cup of coffee in bed.

What gives you hope for a better world?

Cuddling Hildie always raises the spirits. And walks down to the river to admire the community gardens and watch the CityCats go by. ∗

Beer-battered lemon tofu with smashed cucumber salad

Serves 4–6 · Vegan

60 ml (¼ cup) soy sauce or tamari

60 ml (¼ cup) rice wine vinegar

2 heaped tsp Chinese five spice

450 g (1 lb) firm or extra-firm tofu

vegetable oil (or another neutral frying oil), for shallow-frying

cooked or fried rice, to serve

Cucumber salad

4–5 Lebanese cucumbers or 1–2 long cucumbers (about 600 g/1 lb 5 oz)

1 tsp salt

3 garlic cloves, grated or finely chopped

¼–½ long red chilli, thinly sliced (optional)

2 tsp caster (superfine) sugar

60 ml (¼ cup) soy sauce or tamari

2 tbsp rice wine vinegar

2 tbsp sesame oil

Lemon sauce

2 tbsp olive oil

3 garlic cloves, crushed or grated

1 tbsp grated ginger

1 tbsp cornflour (corn starch)

60 ml (¼ cup) freshly squeezed lemon juice

2–3 tbsp honey

salt and white pepper

This has become one of my go-to meals to cook for friends over the last couple of years, inspired by the 'Chinese-for-white-people' classic, lemon chicken. Marinated tofu is dunked in a super-easy beer batter, then fried to crispy perfection and served with a sweet lemon sauce. Served alongside a spicy-sweet smashed cucumber salad and some fluffy white rice or better yet, some speedy fried rice, you have yourself an incredible dinner that everyone will love. The tofu is a little finicky, requiring a marinade, a batter and a final sauce, but it all comes together in pretty good time, and is easily doubled or tripled to serve a big crowd. It's also a great method to nail, then adapt to different flavourings or styles – for example, served with chips and vegan tartar sauce for an excellent vegan to-fish and chips.

Whisk the soy sauce or tamari, rice wine vinegar and Chinese five spice in a small bowl. Tear the tofu into bite-sized pieces (tearing the tofu increases the surface area and creates craggy bits that soak up the marinade better). Lay the tofu chunks on a flat dish or tray with a lip, then evenly pour the marinade over the top. Cover and transfer to the fridge and leave to marinate for 1 hour, or up to 24 hours.

Meanwhile, prepare the cucumber salad by bashing the cucumber with a mallet, rolling pin or a bottle of wine (or anything with a bit of weight) to just crush the cucumber and split it into a few pieces. Slice the bashed cucumber diagonally into 5 mm (¼ in) pieces. Transfer to a colander in the sink and sprinkle with the salt, tossing well to coat. This will help the cucumber to release some of its water content, enabling it to soak up more dressing. Leave the cucumber to sit for 15–30 minutes, while you prepare the rest of the dish.

Whisk the remaining cucumber salad ingredients in a small bowl, adding just half the chilli to begin with, then more to adjust to your taste. The final dressing should be a well-balanced flavour of sweet, salty and sour, so adjust the quantities a little as needed to get the desired flavour. Set the dressing aside until ready to serve.

Prepare the lemon sauce in a small saucepan by heating the olive oil over medium heat. Add the garlic and ginger and fry for 1 minute or until fragrant, then add the cornflour and stir well to combine. Cook for 1 minute, then add the remaining ingredients and 125 ml (½ cup) of water , whisking well for a few minutes to get rid of any cornflour lumps. As the sauce begins to thicken, taste and add a generous seasoning of salt and white pepper. Once it's thick and glossy, turn off the heat and pour the sauce into a serving bowl.

When you're almost ready to serve, heat 2 cm (¾ in) of vegetable oil in a frying pan or shallow saucepan over medium heat. →

Beer-battered lemon tofu with smashed cucumber salad

<u>Beer batter</u>

150 g (1 cup) self-raising flour

3 tbsp sesame seeds

170 ml (⅔ cup) cold beer

Swaps

Gluten free – self-raising flour: cornflour (corn starch); beer: soda water (club soda) or gluten-free beer

Whisk the beer batter ingredients together in a bowl. Remove the tofu from the fridge and give it a final stir through the marinade, then pour off the marinade into the batter. The batter should be a smooth pancake batter–like consistency. Transfer the tofu chunks to the batter and gently stir to coat each piece.

Once the oil is very hot (test with a droplet of the batter; if it sizzles on contact, the oil is ready), working in two or three batches, use tongs to transfer the coated tofu chunks to the pan. Cook the tofu for 1–2 minutes, until golden and crisp, then flip over and continue to cook until golden all over. Transfer to a plate lined with paper towel to drain.

Transfer the cucumber to a serving bowl and pour the dressing over the top, tossing lightly to coat. Serve the tofu chunks alongside rice, the cucumber salad and the lemon sauce, to drizzle on top as you eat, which will ensure the batter retains its crispiness. ✳

Lemon, sage & goat's cheese arancini with sumac aioli

Makes 40–45 small arancini · Gluten Free

50 g (1¾ oz) salted butter

1 large onion, finely diced

4 garlic cloves, minced

1 tsp ground sage (or 1 tbsp finely chopped sage leaves)

zest and juice of 2 lemons (about 1 tbsp zest and 80 ml/⅓ cup lemon juice), plus extra if needed

salt and pepper

440 g (2 cups) arborio rice

1.75 litres (60 fl oz) chicken-style stock, plus extra if needed

120 g (4½ oz) grated parmesan

150 g (5½ oz) soft goat's cheese

vegetable oil (or another neutral oil), for shallow-frying

150 g–300 g (1–2 cups) polenta

Sumac aioli

1 egg

2 garlic cloves, minced

2 tbsp freshly squeezed lemon juice or white vinegar

salt and pepper

250 ml (1 cup) vegetable oil (or another neutral oil)

½ tsp ground sumac

Swaps

Vegan – butter: olive oil; parmesan and goat's cheese: vegan cheese alternatives; egg: aquafaba (soaking liquid from a tin of chickpeas)

Goat's cheese – soft feta, cheddar or extra parmesan

Every single person I've fed these bad boys to has had a quiet moan of ecstasy the minute they eat their first one. They're so damn delicious, and far easier than a traditional stuffed arancini, because the flavour is packed throughout the rice. The soft nuttiness of browned butter, with fragrant lemon zest and creamy soft goat's cheese, is a truly delightful combination. This recipe makes heaps of arancini, so if you don't need that many either halve the recipe, or make half the quantity of arancini and eat the remaining rice as a delicious, citrusy risotto, perfect with some fried mushrooms. When rolling and frying the arancini you need to work with cooled risotto, so you can certainly make it 1–2 days ahead of time. The sumac aioli is quick and a perfect accompaniment, but you could also substitute another aioli or other dipping sauce that you already have.

Melt the butter in a large saucepan over medium heat, until it begins to bubble and separate, with small brown flecks beginning to form. Add the onion, reduce the heat to low and cook for about 10 minutes, until translucent and beginning to brown. Stir through the garlic and cook for 1–2 minutes, until fragrant, then add the sage, lemon zest and plenty of salt and cracked black pepper and stir well to combine. Add the rice and cook, stirring frequently to prevent it sticking to the base of the pan, for 2–3 minutes. Add the stock, 500 ml (2 cups) at a time, stirring well and allowing the liquid to cook down after each addition. After 15–20 minutes, all the stock should be absorbed and the rice should be tender without any chalkiness. If it's still a little chalky, add a little more stock and continue to cook until tender.

Turn off the heat, add the parmesan, goat's cheese and lemon juice and stir well to evenly distribute the ingredients. Cover the pan with a lid and set aside for 5–10 minutes. This will allow the cheese to melt, and I find it helps the risotto become really sticky, meaning your arancini won't fall apart. Taste the risotto and adjust the seasoning or lemon juice if required. Transfer to the fridge to cool.

Meanwhile, make the sumac aioli by whizzing together the egg, garlic, lemon juice and a pinch of salt and pepper in a food processor or small bowl with a whisk. Very slowly drizzle in the oil, while blitzing or whisking, allowing the oil to emulsify. It should gradually thicken as the last of the oil is added. If you're whisking by hand it won't solidify completely, but should be thick enough to use as a dipping sauce. Stir through the sumac and check the seasoning.

Once the risotto is cooled, heat 2–3 cm (¾–1¼ in) of vegetable oil in a small frying pan over medium heat. Pour the polenta into a bowl or dish, then roll the risotto into 2 cm (¾ in) balls and roll them in the polenta. Test the oil with one arancini to check it's hot enough – if it sizzles, the oil is ready.

Fry the arancini in small batches for 4–5 minutes, turning gently a couple of times, until lightly golden with a slightly crunchy outer shell. Using a slotted spoon, transfer the arancini to a plate lined with paper towel to drain. Serve the warm arancini with the sumac aioli. *

Cheat's preserved lemon & chickpea tagine

Serves 6–8 · Vegan · Gluten Free

2 tbsp olive oil

1 large onion, finely diced

2 carrots, finely diced

4 celery stalks, finely diced

6 garlic cloves, finely diced

45 g (1½ oz) ginger, peeled and finely grated

1 long red chilli, finely diced, plus extra if needed

1 tsp ground turmeric

2 tsp fennel seeds

2 tsp cumin seeds

salt and pepper

300 g (10½ oz) dried chickpeas (garbanzo beans), soaked in cold water overnight and drained (or 4 x 400 g/14 oz tins chickpeas, rinsed and drained)

750 ml–1 litre (3–4 cups) vegetable stock (use 1–2 cups if using tinned chickpeas)

1 tsp bicarbonate of soda (baking soda) (omit if using tinned chickpeas)

170 ml (⅔ cup) coconut cream

300 g (10½ oz) green beans, trimmed

cooked rice, quinoa, pearl couscous or pearl barley, to serve

parsley or coriander (cilantro) leaves, to serve

Quick preserved lemons

2 large or 3 small lemons

2 tsp salt

2 tbsp caster (superfine) sugar

This tagine is unlike anything I've ever made before. It's incredibly flavourful and packed to the brim with aromatics. The flavours are inspired by the turmeric, lemon and ginger tea that two of my greatest mates always make whenever anyone is sick. This punchy stew captures some of that wholesome taste and would similarly make a great sinus-clearer comfort food for someone under the weather. The cheat's preserved lemon is a great hack for making preserved lemons quickly, without waiting weeks for homemade or spending half your rent money on a jar from the shops. If you already have some, you can skip the first step and substitute preserved lemons, finely chopped from the jar. You could also use tinned chickpeas at a pinch, if you don't have time to soak dried ones – just note the slight changes to the ingredients and method if doing so.

To make the quick preserved lemons, peel the lemons using a vegetable peeler, then slice the peel into small pieces. Using a knife, remove the pith, as best you can, and discard. If you're using small lemons, there might not be much pith, so don't worry too much about removing it. Chop the lemon flesh into chunks, removing and discarding any seeds as you go. Place the chopped skin and flesh, along with the salt, sugar and 170 ml (⅔ cup) of water in a small saucepan. Cook over low heat for 20–40 minutes, until the water has almost evaporated and the mixture has a jammy texture.

Meanwhile, add the olive oil to a large tagine or heavy-based saucepan, along with the onion, carrot and celery. Cook over medium heat, stirring frequently, for 20 minutes or until the veggies are reduced and starting to caramelise. Add the garlic, ginger and chilli and cook for a further 5 minutes. Add the spices, along with some salt and pepper, and stir well to combine. Cook for 1–2 minutes, then add the chickpeas, 750 ml (3 cups) of the vegetable stock, the bicarbonate of soda and most of the preserved lemon mix, reserving a little to the side to add later if needed. Bring the tagine to a slow simmer and cook, covered, for 30–45 minutes, until the chickpeas are tender. If the chickpeas are particularly large you may need to cook the tagine for longer and add the remaining stock. If you're using tinned chickpeas, start with just 250 ml (1 cup) of vegetable stock and omit the bicarbonate of soda.

Once the chickpeas are almost tender, taste the mixture and add extra salt, chilli or preserved lemon, as required. Add the coconut cream and cook, uncovered, for a further 15 minutes. Give the tagine a final taste and adjust the seasoning if needed. Finally, add the beans and cook for a final couple of minutes, until they're just tender, but still nice and crunchy.

Serve the tagine hot with rice, quinoa, pearl couscous or pearl barley, topped with some parsley or coriander leaves. ✳

Swaps

Carrots – capsicums (bell peppers), zucchini (courgettes) or another sturdy vegetable

Celery or onion – leek or fennel

Coconut cream – oat cream or extra stock

Fennel seeds – caraway seeds or extra cumin seeds

Green beans – broccoli, broccolini, zucchini (courgettes), shredded kale, cabbage or spinach

Lemon pastéis de nata

Makes 24–30

300 g (2 cups) plain (all-purpose) flour, plus extra if needed and for dusting

185 ml (¾ cup) ice-cold water, plus extra if needed

250 g (9 oz) salted butter, very soft, stirred in a bowl

Custard

230 g (1 cup) caster (superfine) sugar

8 egg yolks

40 g (⅓ cup) cornflour (corn starch)

¼ tsp ground cinnamon

1 tsp vanilla essence

685 ml (2¾ cups) milk

juice of 1 lemon (about 2 tbsp)

Every time I eat pastéis de nata (Portuguese custard tarts) I am mentally transferred to a melancholy, rather lonely week or two I spent in Lisbon a few years ago. Everyone in the city seemed to be so full of life and I was depressed, struggling with terrible insomnia and very confused as to why I thought spending three months travelling alone would help. That sounds like not a good memory, but the silver lining was the routine I followed every day while I was there, to hunt down a new pastry shop, buy two or three pastries, then find a good park to sit in and spend hours reading my book. When I think back on that time I don't remember the loneliness, so much as that first, buttery bite into the best pastries in the world.

These custard tarts are time intensive and a bit complex, I won't lie to you. But they're worth every second, and the batch makes enough that it'll feel worth it at the end. The next time you have a free morning and a baking itch, give them a go. Just make sure they're eaten fresh that day. You can store the pastry and custard in the fridge for 3–4 days if you want to make small batches each day.

Combine the flour and ice-cold water in a bowl and mix with a fork to form a scraggy dough. Use your hands to knead the dough, pressing and folding it into itself for 3–5 minutes. After this time, it should change consistency and become pliable and soft, but shouldn't stick to your hands. Add a little extra flour or water if it's too sticky or too dry. Bring the dough into a ball and dust with some flour, then cover with a tea towel and leave to rest for 10 minutes. After this time it should have relaxed and be easy to roll out and work with.

Generously flour a clean work surface and roll the dough into a large thin square, about 40–50 cm (16–20 in). It will take a few minutes, but it's really important to get the dough very thin. Use a plastic spatula to carefully spread one-third of the soft butter across the left two thirds of the dough square, leaving a 1 cm (½ in) border around the edge and creating a thin, even spread across the dough.

Lift up the un-buttered corners of the dough, using a spatula to help if it's sticking a little, and fold it over the middle buttered dough. Pick up the remaining unfolded edges and fold them into the middle, so that you now have a thin, long rectangle. Fold this dough rectangle over itself, to make a shorter rectangle. Dust the work surface and the dough again with a little flour. If it's a very hot day you might want to return the dough to the fridge for 10 or so minutes. Otherwise, move straight on to repeating the process of rolling the rectangle into another square, then repeating the buttering and folding. What you're essentially doing is creating paper-thin distinct layers of dough and butter which, when cooked, will create crispy pastry that shatters beautifully. →

Finally, roll the dough again into a square (it doesn't need to be quite as large at this stage) and spread the remaining butter over the entire dough. Starting at the edge closest to you, roll the dough into a tight log. Cut any overhanging bits at the ends, then cut the log into 3–4 pieces. Wrap each log in plastic wrap and chill in the fridge for about 4 hours, or overnight, until very firm. If you're short on time you can speed this time up by resting the dough in the freezer.

Next prepare the custard. Whisk together the sugar, egg yolks, cornflour, cinnamon and vanilla in a large bowl until smooth.

Heat the milk in a saucepan over medium–low heat, whisking occasionally, until small bubbles appear and it begins to steam a little. Once the milk is close to boiling, take it off the heat and slowly drizzle it into the egg-yolk mixture, whisking constantly as you do. Once all the milk has been incorporated and the mixture is frothy, pour it into the saucepan and return to low heat.

Whisk constantly for a few minutes, until the mixture begins to thicken and coats the back of a spoon. Pour the custard back into the bowl and gently whisk in the lemon juice. Cover with plastic wrap over the surface of the custard (to prevent it developing a film), or put it in an airtight container, and refrigerate until cool.

When you are ready to cook, preheat the oven to 250°C (480°F) fan-forced.

Lightly dust a work surface with flour and cut the dough logs into 5 mm (¼ in) thick slices. Roll out the slices into thin discs about 6 cm (2½ in) in diameter, then press into muffin tin holes so that the pastry comes up the sides, creating little bowls. Don't worry about trimming off the edges. If it's a hot day, or you're still waiting for the oven to heat up, put the tins in the fridge or freezer for 10 minutes. It's important that the butter in the pastry isn't allowed to soften.

Once you're ready to cook, scoop a tablespoon of the custard into each pastry shell, then transfer to the middle shelf of the oven and bake for 15–20 minutes, until the pastry is crisp and golden and the custard is browned. Leave the tarts in the tins for 5–10 minutes, then transfer to a wire rack to cool.

The tarts are best eaten a little warm, and definitely the same day. You can store the pastry and custard in the fridge for up to 2 days, and make a batch fresh each morning, if you like. ❊

Lemon & rosemary cake with mascarpone cream

Makes 1 x 20 cm (8 in) cake

145 g (⅔ cup) caster (superfine) sugar

zest and juice of 2 lemons (about
1 tbsp zest and 80 ml/⅓ cup juice)

150 g (5½ oz) unsalted butter,
chopped and softened

125 ml (½ cup) olive oil

2 eggs

250 g (1 cup) natural yoghurt

½ tsp salt

1 tbsp rosemary leaves, finely chopped

300 g (2 cups) self-raising flour

Mascarpone cream

250 ml (1 cup) double-thickened
(dollop) cream

1 tsp vanilla essence

85 g (⅔ cup) icing (confectioners')
sugar, sifted

250 g (1 cup) mascarpone, at room
temperature

Swaps

*Lemon – lime, orange, blood orange,
tangerines or mandarins*

The rosemary in this cake is subtle but it brings an interesting edge to what is otherwise a great, but simple, butter cake. You can serve it the day it's iced as a beautiful dessert or birthday cake, or keep the mascarpone separate and simply serve it warm, with the cream on the side as a simple dessert, perhaps with some fresh fruit such as peaches and raspberries. Although it's wonderful with lemon, this cake works with any citrus. I particularly love to sub in blood oranges for the few weeks a year they're around at the markets.

Preheat the oven to 180°C (350°F) fan-forced and generously grease or line a 20 cm (8 in) round cake tin with baking paper.

Use your fingers to rub together the sugar and lemon zest in a large mixing bowl until the zest releases some oil and smells beautifully fragrant. Add the butter, lemon juice and olive oil, and use electric beaters to mix for a couple of minutes, until the mixture is light and fluffy.

Add the eggs, and beat again for 1 minute. Don't worry if the mixture splits a bit at this point, it'll come back together when you add the flour. Stir through the yoghurt, salt and rosemary, until well combined, then add the flour and fold it through the mixture.

Pour the batter into the prepared baking tin, then transfer to the oven and bake for 35–45 minutes, until the cake is just set and a skewer inserted into the centre comes out clean. Allow the cake to cool for a few minutes, then remove from the tin and allow it to cool completely on a wire rack.

To make the mascarpone cream, use electric beaters to whip the cream, vanilla and icing sugar in a bowl until the mixture is just beginning to thicken. Add the mascarpone (soften it a little in the microwave, if necessary) and whip again to combine, until the mixture is thick and pillowy, but stopping before stiff peaks form. Serve the icing generously mounted and swirled onto the completely cooled cake, or alongside individual pieces. I like to top the cake with whatever fruit or flowers I have around, but it's perfect just as it is. ✳

Mushrooms

Recipes

Anywhere red meat is traditionally used, mushrooms can find a happy home as a substitute. These recipes take some of those classic meat-based ideas – including souvlaki, stroganoff, savoury mince and meatballs – and transforms them into flavourful plant-based renditions. Mushrooms lendthemselves well to ingredients that complement and draw out their inherent umami, and need to be seasoned well to achieve their full impact.

With Yichi, Anne, Clare, baby Joe and Dylan

Describe your household

Clare, Dylan and baby Joe live upstairs, and Anne and Yichi live downstairs. We are all busy with different comings and goings, and we like to get together to chat in the garden.

Do you share food as a household? How often and what does that involve?

We share food from our garden and keep our produce on the verandah to share. Someone will always have vegetables that need using, or some milk to share for coffee.

What's your favourite way to cook/eat mushrooms?

We love chucking mushrooms in the pan, along with eggs and greens from our garden. Delicious!

What does a typical Saturday morning in your house look like?

Anne gets up and goes to the markets, and often drops by Musgrave Park pool for baby Joe's swimming lesson on the way home. After that we are all ready for the sourdough fruit bread she buys in bulk.

What do you love about living in a share house generally, or about this house in particular?

We love having our 'village' right here in the house with us, and that's really important for baby Joe growing up. People say this house has a 'holiday' feel, which means they come over for a tea or a swim and don't end up leaving.

What gives you and your housemates hope for a better world?

We get a lot of strength from our local community, and try to get active supporting political candidates who truly represent us. Joe is going through a 'posting' stage, so he loves leafletting for our local Greens candidate. ✳

Marinated mushroom yiros 'meat'

Serves 4–6 · Gluten Free

60 ml (¼ cup) olive oil, plus extra
for drizzling

2 tsp ground sumac

1 tsp ground coriander

1 tsp ground cumin

2 tsp garlic powder

2 tsp smoky paprika

1 tsp dried dill (or 1 tbsp chopped
dill fronds)

1 heaped tbsp tomato paste
(concentrated purée)

1 tbsp barbecue sauce

250 g (1 cup) natural yoghurt

1 tbsp soy sauce or tamari

1 tbsp balsamic vinegar

salt and pepper

1 kg (2 lb 3 oz) mixed mushrooms
(shiitake, oyster and shimeji work
wonderfully, but plain old buttons
are fine too), roughly chopped

Swaps

Vegan – yoghurt: coconut yoghurt

Cooking these mushrooms on a screaming-hot barbecue not only creates a delicious flavour, it also cooks them quickly and turns them a little gnarly, giving them a similar texture to traditional yiros meat. Serve the marinated mushrooms alongside warm pitas, grilled haloumi, tzatziki, tomato, lettuce, onion and pickles, ready to assemble into wraps. Alternatively, you can serve the mushrooms with some salads and bread as part of a bigger barbecue spread. If you want to bulk up the mushroom mix, a sliced onion or two makes a nice addition and will help the mix stretch further.

Combine all of the ingredients except the mushrooms in a bowl, stirring until well combined to form a thick marinade. Taste to check the balance of flavours is to your liking – it should taste a little spicy and slightly sweet with a nice hum – and adjust the seasoning as needed. Place the mushrooms in a large bowl, spoon in half the marinade and toss well to combine. Allow the mushrooms to marinate for 20 minutes, or up to a few hours in the fridge.

Preheat a barbecue grill (or a large cast-iron frying pan) to its maximum temperature. Add the marinated mushrooms and use tongs to spread them across the barbecue in an even layer so the heat reaches a maximum surface. Drizzle with a little olive oil and cook, undisturbed, for 5–10 minutes, then use a spatula to stir the mushrooms, scraping any pieces that are starting to stick. Cook for another 10–15 minutes, moving the mushrooms around every few minutes (it's important not to move them too much or they won't turn golden and crisp). If you're cooking the mushrooms in a pan, cook them in batches to achieve maximum golden crispiness.

Once the mushrooms have shrunk considerably and look nice and browned, scoop them into a bowl, pour over the remaining marinade and stir well. Serve the mushrooms as you would in traditional yiros or as part of a barbecue feast. ✳

Creamy mushroom pie
with mashed potato top

Serves 4–6

20 g (1 cup) dried mushrooms (porcini or shiitake work well)

500 ml (2 cups) boiling water

50 g (1¾ oz) salted butter

1 onion, diced

200 g (7 oz) parsnips, diced

5 garlic cloves, minced

½ tsp dried tarragon

½ tsp dried thyme

1 tsp smoky paprika

1 tbsp wholegrain mustard

salt and pepper

2 tbsp tomato ketchup

3 heaped tbsp plain (all-purpose) flour

500 g (1 lb 2 oz) button or Swiss brown mushrooms, roughly chopped

150 g (5½ oz) oyster mushrooms, thinly shredded

250 ml (1 cup) chicken-style stock

1 x 400 g (14 oz) tin lentils, rinsed and drained

160 g (⅔ cup) sour cream

Mashed potato topping

1.25 kg (2 lb 12 oz) potatoes, peeled and chopped into 2 cm (¾ oz) chunks

salt and pepper

50 g (1¾ oz) salted butter, chopped

185 ml (¾ cup) milk

100 g (1 cup) grated cheddar

1 tbsp olive oil

With a luscious, creamy gravy, three varieties of mushrooms bringing a serious umami punch and a soft mashed potato top, this pie is comfort-food heaven. I love the chunks of parsnip throughout, and the lentils make it nice and filling. The mushroom mix has some stroganoff energy from the subtle mustard flavour and sour cream. You could absolutely throw in any sad-looking vegetables you need to use up in this pie – peas, spinach or other leafy greens would be particularly nice, added right at the end.

Start by placing the potato for the mashed potato topping in a large saucepan and covering with cold water. Season with a heaped teaspoon of salt, then bring to the boil over medium heat and cook for about 20 minutes or until super soft when poked with a fork. Drain and transfer to a large bowl and add the butter, milk, cheese and a little salt and pepper. Mash for about 1 minute, until almost smooth. Take care not to over-mash the potato or it will turn to glue – a few lumps are fine.

Meanwhile, place the dried mushrooms in a bowl or container and cover with the boiling water. Cover the bowl or seal the container and let stand for 10 minutes.

Place the butter, onion and parsnip in your largest ovenproof frying pan or low-sided cast-iron pan. If you don't have either, just cook the filling in a large frying pan, then transfer to a baking dish before baking. Cook the veggies over medium heat for about 10 minutes, letting them sweat out some of their water, until starting to caramelise.

Strain the mushrooms, reserving their soaking liquid, then finely chop and add them to the pan, along with the garlic. Stir well and cook for 3–4 minutes, then add the dried herbs, paprika, mustard, 1 teaspoon of pepper, the ketchup and flour. Stir the vegetables well to coat them in the mixture and cook for 1–2 minutes (don't worry if things start to stick to the base of the pan a little). Add the mushrooms (in batches if your pan isn't big enough), the reserved soaking liquid and the stock, and cook, stirring the mixture well to help the liquid deglaze the pan, for 5–10 minutes, until the mushrooms have shrunk and the mixture is starting to thicken. Finally, add the lentils and sour cream, stirring through well. Season with salt and pepper to taste, and cook, stirring frequently, for 5 minutes. Turn off the heat and let the filling cool a little.

Preheat the oven to 200°C (400°F) fan-forced.

Blob the potato on top of the mushroom filling and use a spatula to spread it out evenly. You can make a criss-cross pattern over the top by scraping a fork through the potato. Drizzle over the olive oil and bake the pie for 10–15 minutes, until golden and bubbling. ✳

Mushroom meatballs with harissa sugo

Serves 6–8 · Vegan · Gluten Free

500 g (1 lb 2 oz) mushrooms (any variety), roughly chopped

300 g (10½ oz) firm tofu, roughly chopped

1 onion, sliced

60 ml (¼ cup) olive oil or vegetable oil

salt and pepper

3 garlic cloves, peeled

20 pitted kalamata olives

80 g (½ cup) dates, pitted and roughly chopped

2 tsp ground cumin

1 tbsp tahini

1 flax or chia egg (see Note; or use 1 egg, if not vegan)

60 g (2 oz) panko or fresh breadcrumbs (or use gluten-free breadcrumbs)

Harissa sugo

60 ml (¼ cup) olive oil

1 onion, finely diced

3 garlic cloves, finely diced

1–2 tbsp harissa paste (more if you like it spicy)

1 heaped tsp curry powder or garam masala

1 tsp cumin seeds, crushed lightly using a mortar and pestle, or roughly chopped

1 tsp ground coriander

250 ml (1 cup) vegetable stock

2 x 400 g (14 oz) tins crushed tomatoes

1 tbsp freshly squeezed lemon juice

salt and pepper

I first made this dish while cooking two Ottolenghi recipes and I realised halfway through I didn't have all the required ingredients. Instead of a trip to a supermarket I decided to merge the recipes into one. The finished dish looks very much like Italian meatballs, but the flavours are Middle Eastern. I love the warm hum of spice going on here, and adore any excuse to create a 'meat-like' texture with zero animal products. A great dish to serve to those who think vegan food can't be incredible! I love this served alongside some flatbreads, grilled haloumi or vegetables, crispy roasted chickpeas, sautéed greens or salad and your favourite dips and condiments for a super-special meal. It's also great just with rice.

Preheat the oven to 220°C (430°F) fan-forced. Line two large baking trays with baking paper.

Spread the mushroom, tofu and onion across one of the prepared trays. Drizzle over a little of the olive oil and season lightly with salt and pepper. Roast for 30–40 minutes, stirring halfway through, until the mushrooms have shrunk and the tofu and onion are browned. Roasting the ingredients draws out their water content and will ensure that your meatballs aren't soggy and hold a nice texture.

Transfer the roasted ingredients to a food processor and add the remaining ingredients except the remaining oil. Blitz to form a thick, chunky paste, similar to a falafel mix (it's important to retain some texture). If you only have a blender, hold back from including the breadcrumbs and half the roasted ingredients. Chop them by hand into a chunky crumb, then combine with the breadcrumbs and veggie paste in a bowl. Taste and check it is well seasoned.

Use your hands to roll the mixture into about 20 balls, then transfer to the other baking tray, with space between each meatball. Drizzle over the remaining olive oil and bake for 20–30 minutes, turning halfway through cooking, until firm (but not completely dry), with a lovely colour.

As the meatballs cook, prepare the harissa sugo. Heat the olive oil and onion in a frying pan over medium heat and cook, stirring frequently, for about 10 minutes, until the onion has softened and caramelised a little. Add the garlic, harissa paste and spices and stir well. Cook for 3–4 minutes, until the mixture is sizzling and smelling beautifully fragrant. Pour in the stock and tomatoes and bring to the boil, then reduce the heat to a low simmer and cook for a further 5 minutes. Add the lemon juice, then taste and adjust the seasoning if necessary.

Pour the sugo into a serving dish (or keep it in your frying pan) and gently position the meatballs on top. I don't like to cook them in the sauce, as it will cause the meatballs to break down and become very soft. You could serve this with an extra drizzle of olive oil and some fresh herbs or cumin seeds to garnish, if you like, or serve as is. ✳

Note: To make 1 flax or chia egg, combine 1 tablespoon ground flaxseeds (linseeds) or chia seeds with 2–3 tablespoons of water and stand for 10 minutes or until thickened.

Leek cacio e pepe risotto with seared pickled mushrooms

Serves 4–6 · Gluten Free

50 g (1¾ oz) salted butter

1 large leek, white and pale green parts, finely chopped (save the green top to make stock)

5 garlic cloves, thinly sliced or minced

330 g (1½ cups) arborio rice

1 litre (34 fl oz) vegetable stock, plus extra if needed

150 g (5½ oz) crème fraîche, plus extra to serve

100 g (1 cup) grated parmesan

salt and pepper

thyme sprigs, to serve (optional)

Seared pickled mushrooms

500 g (1 lb 2 oz) mixed mushrooms (I like to use button, shimejis, oyster, shiitake and king oysters), roughly chopped

2 tbsp olive oil, plus extra for drizzling

salt

2 tbsp white wine vinegar

1 tsp sugar

Swaps

Vegan – butter: olive oil; crème fraîche: oat cream or cashew cheese; parmesan: vegan parmesan or 3 tbsp nutritional yeast

I don't generally love risotto. Along with mint chocolate–flavoured things (I'm sorry), it's one of the few foods in the world that I would generally pass up. But one night I had a weird craving and this recipe came to be. This super creamy and luscious risotto is inspired by cacio e pepe pasta, and topped with zingy pickled mushrooms that make it more interesting than your average mushroom risotto. I think it makes for a pretty lovely dinner plus it comes together in no time. If you find fancy mushrooms, such as oysters and shimejis, for a good price, this is a great way to cook them.

Melt the butter in a large, heavy-based saucepan or deep frying pan over medium heat. Add the leek and cook, stirring frequently, for about 10 minutes, until starting to brown. Stir through the garlic, then add the rice and stir well to combine. Cook for about 2 minutes, then pour in half the vegetable stock. Reduce the heat to medium–low and bring to a very gentle simmer. Continue to cook the rice, adding the remaining stock and 375 ml (1½ cups) of water in 125 ml (½ cup) quantities, stirring gently after each addition and waiting for the stock or water to absorb before adding more liquid.

Meanwhile, to make the seared pickled mushrooms, place a large frying pan over high heat until screaming hot. Add half the mushroom and 1 tablespoon of the olive oil plus a pinch of salt, and cook, undisturbed, for 2–3 minutes, then gently toss or flip the mushroom and cook for another 3 minutes or until reduced and golden. Don't over-stir the mushrooms, otherwise they won't brown properly and you won't achieve that smoky flavour. Transfer the mushroom to a bowl and repeat with the remaining mushroom and olive oil.

In a separate small bowl, combine the white wine vinegar, sugar and ½ teaspoon of salt, and stir until the sugar and salt have dissolved. Pour the pickling liquid over the mushroom and toss well to coat. Cover the bowl with a plate or some foil to keep warm until you're ready to serve. As they sit, the mushroom will release some extra juices to combine with the pickling liquid.

Once all the liquid has been added to the risotto, taste a little rice to check that it's almost cooked. If not, add a little extra stock and continue to cook until the rice is al dente.

Add the crème fraîche, parmesan, a pinch of salt and a very generous portion of freshly cracked black pepper (about 1 teaspoon) to the risotto and stir through. Taste and add more seasoning, if needed. Turn off the heat and cover the pan, letting it sit for a couple of minutes to finish cooking.

Serve the risotto in bowls, topped with some pickled mushroom and a drizzle of the pickling liquid. Add a little crème fraîche and some extra olive oil or seasoning as desired. Finish with a couple of sprigs of thyme, if you like, and serve. ✳

Savoury mince

Serves 4–6 · Vegan · Gluten Free

2 tbsp olive oil

1 large onion, finely diced

2 carrots, finely diced

500 g (1 lb 2 oz) mushrooms
(any variety), finely diced

5 garlic cloves, minced

2 tsp curry powder (preferably Keen's)

1 heaped tbsp beef-style gravy powder

2 tbsp tomato paste
(concentrated purée)

1 x 400 g (14 oz) tin black beans

250 ml (1 cup) vegetable stock

salt and pepper

chilli sauce, to taste (optional)

150 g (1 cup) frozen peas

Swaps

*Black beans – kidney beans, haricot
beans or borlotti beans*

*Curry powder – DIY spice mix
of ground cumin, coriander and
turmeric, and salt*

*Gravy powder – 1 stock cube or 1 tsp
stock powder plus 1 tbsp plain
(all-purpose) flour*

*Onion or carrots – celery, fennel,
capsicum (bell peppers), zucchini
(courgettes), brussels sprouts or
pumpkin (winter squash)*

*This veggie mince is a go-to make-ahead meal, perfect for feeding a crowd
or for brekkie, lunch or dinner. It's cheap and delicious and makes a great
pie filling, topping for mashed or jacket potatoes, or a tasty addition to
a fried egg on toast. There's something simple and nostalgic about the
hum of spice and savouriness that the gravy powder and curry powder
bring here that reminds me of school camp as a kid. Feel free to add an
extra tin of beans to bulk up the servings, and add any finely chopped
veggies you have looking a bit sad in the crisper.*

Heat the olive oil in a large frying pan or saucepan over medium heat. Add
the onion and carrot and cook, stirring frequently, for about 10 minutes,
until starting to caramelise. Increase the heat to high, add the mushroom and
cook, stirring occasionally, for 5–8 minutes, until the liquid released from the
mushroom has mostly evaporated. Add the garlic, curry powder, gravy powder
and tomato paste, stir well to combine, then cook for 3–4 minutes, until
everything is well coated and the mixture is fragrant.

Meanwhile, blend the black beans and their soaking liquid in a food processor
or with a stick blender until broken up into a chunky paste. You can also just
mash the beans with a potato masher or fork until they're roughly crushed.

Stir the mashed beans and vegetable stock through the mushroom mixture
and check the seasoning. You shouldn't need much salt because the gravy
powder and stock will be quite salty, but you could add some pepper or a
splash of chilli sauce if you like spice. Bring the mixture to a simmer and cook
for 5 minutes or until slightly thickened, then add the frozen peas and mix well.
Turn off the heat and allow the peas to cook in the residual heat but don't let
them become mushy – their vibrancy is important.

Serve the mince warm with whatever accompaniments you like. ✳

Onion

The onion really is the epitome of a background vegetable.
It features in just about all of the savoury dishes in this book,
but in this chapter, onion is pickled, sautéed or caramelised to
put it front and centre. Most of the dishes here are very pantry
friendly, perfect for the end of the week when you only have
a few scrappy onions left and still want to make something
wholesome for dinner. For those who can't digest onions,
leeks, fennel, celery or capsicums (bell peppers) make good
replacements in these recipes, and most throughout the book.

With Anna, Jordan, India and Fia

Describe your household

Anna (Cancer) is a Native Title researcher; Fia (Virgo) works as a journalist and recently moved here from Naarm for a job; India (Aquarius) works from home for the New Zealand Department of Conservation; Jordan (Scorpio) is a visual artist who makes abstract works from beeswax and pigment; Percy (Aries) sleeps most of the time, looks at bugs and is skilled at picking out only the more expensive biscuits in his food mix. He is also a cat.

We love living together and coming home to our inner-city paradise. Plants dappled throughout each room are key to the fresh, serene, lush vibe. We're most often found sharing a wine in the olive tree courtyard, interrogating people about their star signs.

Do you share food as a household? How often and what does that involve?

We share meals intuitively, depending on how everyone's week flows. Often we come home and someone is already making a generous meal with an offer to share. While we do have solo cooking ventures, the most fun is when everyone's ideas and ingredients turn into an impromptu potluck feast. We would cringe at having a rigid structure around mealtimes – planned meals at set times would be a nightmare. We believe it's better to share a wine than drink alone.

What do you love about living in a share house generally, or about this house in particular?

Okay let's get deep. It's about sharing space with our chosen family. It's special to be able to see how others live, and to have such a casual but intimate relationship with good people. You adopt people into your life, they're not just those you live with but those you create a wider community with. The whole is greater than the sum of its parts. We love our home.

What gives you and your housemates hope for a better world?

Young people are inspiring in how they care about the world and engage in politics to a deeper level than we did at their age. We share similar political ideals, which helps. We love meeting people who are active and engaged in fixing broken systems, practising kindness and generosity, and having conversations about building better alternatives. Our community gives us a lot of hope. *

Beans with tahini cream & pickled onions

Serves 4 as a main, or 8–10 as a side · Vegan · Gluten Free

2 tbsp olive oil, plus extra for drizzling

1 onion (any variety), diced

4 garlic cloves, minced

2 x 400 g (14 oz) tins cannellini beans, rinsed and drained

2 bay leaves

250 ml (1 cup) vegetable stock

salt and pepper

juice of ½ lemon (about 1 tbsp)

2 tomatoes, diced

½ bunch of parsley, leaves picked and chopped

Pickled onion

1 large red onion, halved and very thinly sliced

60 ml (¼ cup) red wine vinegar

2 tbsp apple cider vinegar

1 heaped tsp salt

1 heaped tbsp sugar

Tahini cream

65 g (¼ cup) tahini

60 ml (¼ cup) olive oil

juice of ½ lemon (about 1 tbsp)

salt and white pepper

Swaps

Cannellini beans – butter (lima) beans or chickpeas (garbanzo beans)

Tomatoes – cucumber, avocado or roasted vegetables such as capsicums (bell peppers) or eggplants (aubergines)

Served warm or cold, this dish is made almost entirely from pantry basics but looks and tastes like something with more luxury. Onion features both within the beans mix, providing the sweet depth of flavour that it does so well, and also sits atop the finished dish, providing a shock of beautiful pink and a wonderfully sweet and sour pickle flavour. If you have time, make the pickled onions ahead as they are best left to pickle longer – preferably an extra hour or two –and served cold. You'll need less than the recipe makes, so use the leftovers in sandwiches or salads (see page 218) over the next week or two. The same pickling method can also be used to quick-pickle other veggies such as zucchini, cucumber, cauliflower, mushrooms, radishes or cabbage.

To make the pickled onion, place the onion in a small bowl or jar. Heat the remaining pickle ingredients and 60 ml (¼ cup) of water in a small saucepan over medium heat, until they begin to slowly simmer. Pour the hot vinegar mixture over the onion and ensure that the slices are submerged. Cover the bowl with plastic wrap or screw the lid on the jar, then transfer to the fridge until ready to serve.

Heat the olive oil in a frying pan over low heat, then add the onion and garlic and cook, stirring frequently, for 5–10 minutes, until soft and translucent. Add the beans, bay leaves and vegetable stock and gently stir to combine. Season with a pinch of salt and pepper, bring to a gentle simmer and cook for about 10 minutes, until most of the stock has evaporated.

Meanwhile, make the tahini cream by whisking together the ingredients and 60 ml (¼ cup) of water in a bowl to form a thick, very light-coloured cream. Taste and adjust the seasoning until you can taste a nice hum of salt. The cream will taste a little bitter but will complement the sweet and fragrant beans beautifully. Spread the tahini cream across the base of a serving dish or plate.

Once the beans are done, turn off the heat, add the lemon juice and leave to cool a little, then add the tomato and most of the parsley and toss to combine. Spoon the bean mixture over the tahini cream, then sprinkle over the remaining parsley. Finish by arranging a few tablespoons of the cooled pickled onion on top and drizzling the whole dish with a little extra olive oil and pinch of salt.

Serve the dish warm or at room temperature with flatbread as a perfect starter, or add another salad or two for a lovely light dinner.

The leftover pickled onion will store for weeks in the fridge. ✻

Caramelised onion & mozzarella stuffed pockets

Serves 4–6

1 scant tsp instant dried yeast

185 ml (¾ cup) warm water

300 g (2 cups) plain (all-purpose) flour or bread flour

1 tsp salt

2 tbsp olive oil

50 g (1¾ oz) active sourdough starter (optional)

rice flour or semolina, for dusting

Onion & mozzarella filling

1 garlic bulb, unpeeled

2 tbsp olive oil, plus extra for drizzling

75 g (2¾ oz) salted butter

500 g (1 lb 2 oz) onions, thinly sliced

2 tbsp brown sugar

2 tbsp red wine vinegar

flaky sea salt and pepper

250 g (9 oz) buffalo mozzarella, torn into small chunks

Swaps

Vegan – mozzarella: vegan cheese, roasted vegetables or ajvar (a roasted capsicum condiment); butter: olive oil

These babies are inspired by an onion bread a nice Italian joint down the road from my old house used to make. Everything else there was super expensive, but these humble breads were enormous and only cost $7, so my housemates and I used to go there all the time and mostly just eat them. The filling is very simple but delicious, and cooked on a scorching barbecue it captures a similar smokiness that you might get from a wood-fired pizza oven. What you mustn't skimp on though is the cooking process for the onions – cooking them incredibly slowly is essential to achieving the desired melt-in-your-mouth effect. Serve with some greens or a salad and you've got yourself dinner, or take these to your mates' place as part of a spread. If you have an active sourdough starter, I recommend adding a few tablespoons into the dough to take it to the next level.

Preheat the oven to 200°C (400°F) fan-forced.

Mix the yeast and warm water together in a large bowl and leave for 10 minutes or until frothy. Add the flour, salt, olive oil and starter (if using) and knead for 5 minutes or until pliable and smooth. Form the dough into a round ball, then cover with a tea towel and leave in a warm place until doubled in size, about 1–3 hours depending on the weather. You can also make the dough a day ahead and leave it in the fridge to prove for 8–24 hours, which will ensure an even tastier and chewier dough (just make sure you allow the dough to come to room temperature before rolling).

Meanwhile, to make the filling, place the garlic bulb in a square of foil and drizzle with the olive oil. Loosely wrap the garlic, then transfer to the oven and roast for 30 minutes or until the garlic is soft. (This can also be done ahead of time while you're cooking something else in the oven.) Set aside to cool.

Melt the butter in a heavy-based saucepan over low heat, add the onion and cook for 40–60 minutes, stirring every 10 minutes, until reduced, golden brown and super silky. Add the brown sugar and red wine vinegar, along with a generous seasoning of flaky salt and cracked black pepper, and cook, stirring frequently, for another 10 minutes. Set the onion aside to cool.

Lightly dust a clean work surface with rice flour or semolina. You can also use plain (all-purpose) flour, but I find the former sticks less to the dough and makes it easier to work with. Split the dough into six even-sized pieces and use your hands to stretch each piece of dough into a circle at least 10 cm (4 in) in diameter. Divide the onion, mozzarella and a slightly squished clove or two of the roasted garlic among the bottom half of each dough circle, then fold over the empty side of the dough and press down to seal the filling. Dust with some extra rice flour or semolina, then transfer to a piece of baking paper. Drizzle the pockets with a little extra olive oil and sprinkle with some flaky salt. Leave the pockets to prove while you preheat a barbecue flat plate to its maximum temperature. →

Carefully transfer the pockets to the barbecue by flipping them from the paper onto the flat plate. Close the lid and cook for 3–5 minutes, until browned, then flip and cook the other side for 2–3 minutes, until the pockets have puffed up and are golden brown. Be careful to avoid tearing the dough, otherwise things can get a little messy. If you don't have a barbecue, you can cook the pockets in the oven. Preheat the oven to its maximum temperature (at least 250°C/480°F), then cook the pockets on a baking tray lined with baking paper for 15–20 minutes, flipping them halfway through cooking.

Leftover roasted garlic will keep in the fridge in an airtight container for up to 1 week, and is beautiful in sauces, marinades or dips. *

A perfect salad with quick-pickled onions & toasted breadcrumbs

Serves 6–8 as a side

1 large red onion, very thinly sliced

60 ml (¼ cup) apple cider vinegar

1 tbsp caster (superfine) sugar

1 tsp salt

3 thick slices good-quality bread, roughly torn

2 tbsp olive oil

salt and pepper

200 g (7 oz) leafy lettuce, such as oak, mesclun or a leaf mix (or use 1 large head of lettuce)

Miso–mayo dressing

1 egg

1 tbsp white vinegar

1 tbsp miso paste

salt and white pepper

125 ml (½ cup) olive oil

Swaps

Gluten free – bread: chopped walnuts or pumpkin seeds (pepitas)

Vegan – egg: 2 tbsp aquafaba (liquid from a tin of chickpeas/garbanzo beans)

Lettuce – shredded kale or blanched greens, such as sugar snaps, dwarf or green beans or broccolini

This salad is simple and uses such humble ingredients, but is super special. Next time your garden's lettuce patch is pumping, or you get your hands on some quality green leaves, this is what you should do with them. The delicious and addictive miso–mayo dressing will make more than you need, so save some for sandwiches or to eat with roast potatoes later in the week. Swap in premade pickled onion, packet breadcrumbs and store-bought mayo mixed with a little miso and extra oil if you want a beautiful salad in less than 5 minutes.

Place the onion in a small bowl or jar. Heat the vinegar, sugar, salt and 60 ml (¼ cup) of water in a small saucepan over low heat until the sugar has dissolved and the mixture is very hot. Pour the pickling liquid over the onion and stir to coat the onion. Cover the bowl with plastic wrap or screw on the lid of the jar, then set aside in the fridge to pickle for at least 30 minutes, and up to a few days ahead.

Blitz the bread chunks in a food processor to form a rough crumb, with most of the pieces roughly the same size. If you don't have a food processor, simply cut the bread into croutons. Tip the breadcrumbs into a frying pan set over medium heat and drizzle over the olive oil. Fry, stirring frequently, for 10 minutes, until they begin to toast and become golden and crunchy. Season with salt and pepper and set aside.

Next, whisk all the ingredients for the miso–mayo dressing except the oil, either by hand or in a food processor. While whisking or blending, drizzle in the olive oil, taking care to add it in a very slow and steady trickle, until the dressing has emulsified and thickened.

Just before you're ready to serve, drizzle the dressing over the lettuce leaves and toss gently. Scatter over the pickled onion (discard the pickling liquid or save it for another salad dressing) and the crunchy breadcrumbs, then gently toss the salad to combine. Serve immediately. ✳

Creamy onion pasta with dill & capers

Serves 4–6 · Vegan

4 onions, thinly sliced

125 ml (½ cup) olive oil

6 garlic cloves, smashed

salt

500 g (1 lb 2 oz) dried pasta
(or 600 g/1 lb 5 oz fresh)

125 ml (½ cup) milk of your choice

3 heaped tbsp nutritional yeast

40 g (¼ cup) toasted pine nuts

juice of ½ lemon (about 1 tbsp)

Dill–caper topping

1 garlic clove, minced

40 g (¼ cup) toasted pine nuts

80 g (½ cup) capers, plus 2 tbsp of
their soaking vinegar

small bunch of dill, fronds chopped

60 ml (¼ cup) olive oil

½ tsp chilli flakes (optional)

salt and pepper

This is a weird and wonderful pasta that was born from my desire to recreate an alfredo-like dish, suitable for vegan mates. To get the sauce to its destined silky texture, a high-powered blender is essential. The fragrant topping is a real winner, and would also be great with mashed or roasted potatoes or atop scrambled eggs or avo toast, so feel free to make extra. Dill is the only thing you might not have on hand and as delightful as it is here, you could sub in parsley or basil or even oregano.

Load the sliced onion into a large heavy-based saucepan, along with the olive oil. Cook, stirring occasionally, over medium heat for 10 minutes or until brown and silky. Add the whole smashed garlic cloves and continue to cook for another 10 minutes or until the onion is well caramelised and the garlic is soft and fragrant. Keep a close eye on it to ensure it doesn't begin to burn, and reduce the heat if needed. Scrape the onion and garlic into a blender. Rinse out the pan, then fill with hot water and bring to a rapid boil, adding a couple of teaspoons of salt.

As the water heats and the onion cools a little, prepare the dill–caper topping by bashing the ingredients using a mortar and pestle. Alternatively, you can just roughly chop the nuts, capers and dill, then mix the ingredients together in a bowl with the garlic, olive oil and caper vinegar. Season with the chilli flakes (if using), salt and pepper, and set aside until ready to serve.

Add the pasta to the boiling water and stir well. Cook for 2 minutes less than the packet instructions.

As the pasta cooks, finish the sauce by adding the milk, nutritional yeast, pine nuts, lemon juice and 1 teaspoon of salt to the blender with the onion, along with about 125 ml (½ cup) of the pasta cooking water. Blend until completely smooth – it should be thick and silky.

Drain the pasta, taking care to reserve 250 ml (1 cup) of the salty, starchy water. Return the pasta to the pan and add the blended sauce, along with most of the pasta cooking water. Stir over medium heat until the sauce coats the pasta and the pasta is al dente, adding some extra cooking water if needed. Taste a piece and add extra seasoning if necessary.

Serve the pasta in bowls, topped with a generous swirl of the topping. ✳

Cheese & onion pie
(with exceptionally easy pastry)

Serves 4–6

30 g (1 oz) salted butter, plus extra
for greasing

800 g (1 lb 12 oz) onions, thinly sliced

125 ml (½ cup) pouring cream

1 egg

1½ tbsp English mustard

1 heaped tsp smoky paprika

1 tsp ground sage (or 2 tsp chopped
sage leaves)

150 g (1½ cups) grated vintage cheddar

salt and pepper

Exceptionally easy pastry

150 g (5½ oz) salted butter

170 ml (⅔ cup) milk, plus extra if
needed

1 tsp English mustard

525 g (3½ cups) plain (all-purpose)
flour, plus extra if needed and for
dusting

1 tsp salt

1 egg, beaten

1 tbsp sesame seeds (optional)

*This pie tastes better than it should, with such simple flavours and a pastry
so easy to make and work with that even the most pastry-hesitant won't be
able to stuff it up. It can take a little longer to prepare than you might like
for a weeknight dinner (unless you slow-cook the onions ahead of time),
but it is pretty hands-off for the most part. The bite from the cheddar and
mustard is important, so don't skimp here and use the sharpest cheddar
you can find. It's delicious hot or at room temperature, making it a great
pie to take to a picnic. It'll also keep for days in the fridge and can be
warmed up to eat later.*

Melt the butter in a large frying pan over medium–low heat, add the onion and
cook, stirring occasionally, for at least 20 minutes, until reduced, caramelised
and incredibly silky. Don't skimp on the time here, as the onion needs to do its
thing and not be rushed. Set the onion aside in a large bowl to cool to room
temperature, then add the remaining ingredients and whisk well to combine.
Season well with salt and pepper and set aside.

Preheat the oven to 200°C (400°F) fan-forced. Line the base of a 20 cm
(8 in) springform cake tin with baking paper and grease the side with butter.
If you don't have a springform tin, a small baking dish will do, but make sure
you line it well to prevent the pastry sticking.

Prepare the pastry by melting the butter and milk in a small saucepan over low
heat. Allow the mixture to almost come to the boil, then turn off the heat and
whisk in the mustard.

Place the flour and salt in a bowl and mix well. Create a well in the flour
and pour in the hot milk mixture. Use a fork to gently whisk the ingredients
together, until you have a sticky dough. Knead lightly with your hands to create
a smooth ball, incorporating a little extra flour or milk if necessary – it should
be a lot softer than other pastry dough, and it shouldn't stick to your hands
much because of all that melted butter. Cut the dough into two pieces, one
about twice as big as the other.

On a lightly floured work surface, use a rolling pin (or a bottle of wine) to roll
out the larger piece of dough into a large circle, about 1–2 mm (1/16–1/8 in) thick,
with a diameter almost double the size of the cake tin. If it's looking too big or
not very circular, use a knife to cut it out into a better shape. Roll the pastry
gently onto the rolling pin and then back out onto the tin, pressing the dough
to fill the tin, with any excess hanging over the top. Patch up any pieces that
tear in the process. Roll out the smaller piece of pastry into a neat circle about
the same size as the tin.

Scoop the onion and cheese filling into the pie shell and spread it out evenly. Gently place the pastry lid on top, then fold any overhanging excess pastry over the lid to seal the pie. You can make it pretty by crimping small folds all the way around the edge, if you like. Brush the top with the beaten egg, sprinkle over the sesame seeds (if using) and use a sharp knife to cut a hole in the lid for steam to escape.

Bake the pie for 35–45 minutes, until the top is a deep golden brown. It's important to cook it long enough for the base to cook, so don't be tempted to remove it at the first sign of colour.

Serve the pie alongside a small array of condiments for dipping, with some salad greens on the side. ✳

Potato

Everyone's favourite vegetable ... whether fried, mashed, baked or boiled, potatoes are a blank canvas, waiting to be salted, sauced, topped and devoured. In my house there's almost always a stack at the bottom of the pantry, and when inspiration is lacking, they make the best base for dinner, simply chopped and roasted in oil with salt and then topped with whatever lurks in the fridge begging to be used. I'm sure you also have your potato staple meals; hopefully these recipes might inspire a new one.

With Sid, Anna Z, Gen and Anna R

Do you share food as a household? How often and what does that involve?

We're pretty communal with most things and love to cook meals for each other. Sometimes it's all in, sometimes it's just the Annas cooking for Sid (all the time*), and Gen, although she hates the term, is an efficient meal prepper.

*Sid always does the dishes.

How do you navigate sharing a kitchen?

We're pretty relaxed with who buys and makes food, and unless someone has a special meal planned we're happy to share. If someone is making dinner they'll generally offer it to the house, and it all kind of balances out in the end. 'If you don't cook you do the dishes', is the closest we get to a roster. Our main challenge is that our fridge is always at 100 per cent capacity. Anna R has roughly three empty jars of feta in there ('I'm going to use the oil!'), Sid has a constant supply of mayo, Anna Z keeps every lemon half in a little container and Genevieve will have some elaborate baked creation tucked away.

What's your favourite way to cook/eat potatoes?

It's not high cuisine, but we have a constant supply of potato gems in the freezer – if we're feeling fancy, we add a homemade sauce on top. In winter, by candlelight, it's mashed potato with veggie roast. We make Spanish tortilla for breakfast with our chickens' eggs when there's nothing left in the fridge. The potato doughnuts in this chapter are fucking unbelievable.

What do you love about living in a share house generally, or about this house in particular?

It's just so nice to have family to come home to at the end of the day. Or wake up to. I think for all of us, share-housing is a hugely social thing, and not just because we can't afford a house (which we can't). Communal living allows you to share your life with friends, and benefit from the mutual support that comes with that (as well as the free gardeners that come with the place aka Anna and Anna). We're a mix of old and newish friends that have fortunately bonded really well. Navigating any shared space can be tricky, especially with a house of creative people who can have conflicting tastes or sprawling messy projects (and there will always be the fridge clean-out debacle), but at the end of the day we're friends and that's the best part of sharing this house together. *

Tiny potatoes with walnuts, raisins & jalapeno jam

Serves 6–8 as a side · Gluten Free

1.5 kg (3 lb 5 oz) potatoes, cut into 1 cm (½ in) cubes

60 ml (¼ cup) olive oil

1 tsp salt

125 g (1 cup) chopped walnuts

100 g (3½ oz) raisins

250 g (1 cup) sour cream

handful of herb leaves, to serve (optional)

Jalapeno jam

2 tbsp cumin seeds

100 g (½ cup) pickled jalapenos, finely chopped

1 tsp smoky paprika

salt and pepper

60 ml (¼ cup) maple syrup

2 tbsp white wine vinegar

Swaps

Vegan – sour cream: vegan aioli, vegan sour cream or cashew cream

Maple syrup – brown or caster (superfine) sugar

Pickled jalapenos – fresh mild chillies or chopped spring onions (scallions)

Raisins – currants, dried cranberries or sultanas (golden raisins)

Walnuts – slivered almonds, pumpkin seeds (pepitas) or sunflower seeds

Its name might sound a tad strange but this potato dish is a delicious crowd-pleaser. Crunchy walnuts and sweet pops of juicy raisins nestle themselves in the crispy potatoes, which are then drowned in sour cream and a spicy, jammy, jalapeno sauce. The textures are incredible and the flavour combination is reminiscent of potato wedges with sour cream and sweet chilli sauce (my favourite pub food). Easily adaptable into a vegan side by swapping the sour cream for a vegan alternative, serve these potatoes at your next barbecue or gathering as part of a spread.

Preheat the oven to 200°C (400°F) fan-forced.

Toss the potato in the olive oil and salt to coat well, then spread them across your two largest baking trays. Bake for 40–50 minutes, flipping the potato halfway through cooking, until they start to look crisp and golden. Evenly scatter over the walnuts and raisins and use a spatula to distribute them throughout the potato. Cook for a final 8–10 minutes, to toast the walnuts and allow the potato to crisp up a little more.

Meanwhile, to make the jalapeno jam, heat a small frying pan over medium heat, add the cumin seeds and toast for 1 minute or until fragrant. Add the jalapeno, paprika, salt and pepper and maple syrup, and cook for 1 minute or until the maple syrup is beginning to bubble, then add the white vinegar and 60 ml (¼ cup) of water. Stir well and let the mixture cook down for a couple of minutes, then remove from the heat and set aside to cool until you're ready to serve.

Stir the sour cream in its pot for a few seconds to help loosen it.

Taste the crispy potato mixture to ensure that it's salty enough, then tip into a large, shallow bowl. Spoon over the sour cream and finish by scooping over the jalapeno jam. Sprinkle over a few herbs, if desired. ✳

Lemon potatoes
& the best black-eyed peas

Serves 4–6 · Vegan · Gluten Free

225 g (8 oz) dried black-eyed peas
(or 3 x 400 g/14 oz tins black-eyed
peas, rinsed and drained)

60 ml (¼ cup) olive oil, plus extra
for drizzling

1 small fennel, finely diced

1 large yellow capsicum (bell pepper),
finely diced

6 garlic cloves, thinly sliced

2 tsp dried oregano

1 tbsp cumin seeds, bashed using a
mortar and pestle or roughly chopped

1 heaped tsp smoky paprika

1 tsp pepper

250 ml (1 cup) white wine

1 litre (34 fl oz) vegetable stock, plus
extra if needed (reduce to 375 ml/
1½ cups if using tinned beans)

1 x 400 g (14 oz) tin crushed tomatoes

salt

1 tbsp red wine vinegar

Lemon potatoes

6 large potatoes, peeled and cut into
bite-sized cubes or slices

1 litre (34 fl oz) vegetable stock

3 bay leaves

4 garlic cloves, smashed with the back
of a knife

1 tbsp rosemary leaves (or 1 tsp dried)

1 tsp dried oregano

125 ml (½ cup) freshly squeezed
lemon juice

salt and pepper

2 tbsp olive oil

My last share house was a minute's walk away from one of Brisbane's favourite Greek restaurants. Naturally, it was our go-to for takeaway, and every time we'd be sure to order an extra serve of lemon potatoes to snack on or incorporate into other meals in the days ahead. This recreation is comfort food at its best, if you ask me. Soft, lusciously lemony potatoes are created by boiling spuds in a simple broth, while the black-eyed peas are rich and packed with flavour. Both elements are beautiful on their own, but together they make a wonderful dinner alongside some crunchy greens. You can use either dried black-eyed peas or tinned, and although they require you to plan ahead, I do find the soaked dried peas to be better because they spend longer cooking in the broth. If you have leftover lemon potatoes, they're incredible in a pasta, with pesto and some crunchy greens.

Place the dried black-eyed peas in a large saucepan or bowl and cover with about 1 litre (34 fl oz) of water. Leave to soak for at least 6 hours. Alternatively, cover with boiling water and leave to soak for 1–2 hours.

Heat the olive oil in a large heavy-based saucepan over medium heat. Add the fennel and capsicum and cook, stirring occasionally, for 10–12 minutes, until caramelised and starting to stick a little. Add the garlic, dried oregano, cumin, paprika and pepper and cook for a further 3–4 minutes. Drain the peas, then add them to the pan along with the white wine and stock. Bring to a gentle simmer and cook for about 1 hour, until the beans are almost tender. If using tinned beans, reduce the cooking time to 10–15 minutes.

Meanwhile, to make the lemon potatoes, place all of the ingredients except the olive oil in a saucepan. Gently stir to combine and ensure that the potato is submerged in the liquid. If necessary, add extra stock or water until the potato is just covered. Place the pan over high heat, cover with a lid and bring to the boil, then remove the lid and reduce the heat a little to prevent the liquid spluttering. Simmer for about 20 minutes, stirring occasionally once enough of the broth has evaporated and the potato is no longer submerged, until the potato can be easily pierced with a fork. By this point, most of the liquid should have evaporated. Drizzle over the olive oil, season with salt and pepper and gently stir to combine. Turn off the heat and cover the pan for at least 10 minutes, or until ready to serve. The potato will stay hot for some time and continue to soak up the liquid, becoming even more soft and tender.

When the black-eyed peas are almost tender, add the crushed tomatoes and an additional 250 ml (1 cup) of stock or water if the pan looks a little dry. Cook for a further 15 minutes until thick. Taste and season with salt and pepper, then stir in the vinegar. Drizzle with a generous amount of olive oil, so the black-eyed peas are glossy and rich.

Swaps

*Black-eyed peas – borlotti beans,
cannellini beans or butter (lima) beans
(adjust the soaking/cooking times as
required)*

*Capsicum (bell pepper) – carrot,
pumpkin (winter squash), zucchini
(courgette) or mushrooms*

Fennel – leek, onion, celery or shallots

Serve the black-eyed peas in a large serving dish, with the lemon potatoes on
top or in another bowl. If you have any leftover cooking liquid, either spoon
it over the potato or be sure to save it and use it in sauces and dips or drizzled
over roasted veggies. ✳

Smoky potato & rosemary bread

Makes 2 loaves · Vegan

3–4 whole potatoes (about 500 g/
1 lb 2 oz), brushed to remove any dirt

675 g (1 ½ lb) bread flour, plus extra
for dusting

135 g (5 oz) spelt flour

600 ml (20½ fl oz) warm water

18 g (¾ oz) salt, plus an extra pinch

150 g (5½ oz) sourdough starter, that's
ready to bake with (or 1 x 7 g/¼ oz
sachet instant dried yeast)

3 tbsp rosemary leaves, roughly
chopped

60 ml (¼ cup) olive oil

2 tbsp honey or maple syrup, plus
extra for drizzling

pepper

*It's all been said before, but bread-making can be the most incredible
meditation. If you, like me, struggle to calm a busy mind, I can't
recommend it enough. The slow, involved process of making sourdough
is not for everyone, but it definitely isn't as difficult as you might think. If
you haven't yet got into baking sourdough, but are keen, I'd recommend
watching some video tutorials online. That's how I taught myself and it's
much easier than reading a recipe. That said, there's much to be learned
from trial and error, so here I've included some of my best tips.*

*I use the scooped-out flesh from whole baked potatoes, as it enables you
to transfer a little of that smoky oven flavour into the final bread. For those
more comfortable with using yeast, I've included that option too, which
also makes a satisfyingly quick loaf you can have ready in a few hours.
Of course you could omit the potato and rosemary and use this recipe
as a base for a regular sourdough, or play around with different flavour
combinations. I've only included the ingredients by weight here, as it's
important to measure things out exactly when making bread.*

Sourdough method

Preheat your oven to its maximum temperature. Place the whole potatoes on
the middle shelf and bake for 1 hour, turning halfway through cooking.

Meanwhile, combine the flours and 550 ml (18½ fl oz) of the water in a
large bowl and use your hands or a fork to form a shaggy dough that's
evenly combined. Set aside to rest, covered with a clean tea towel, for
20–30 minutes. This step helps to hydrate the flour and begin to develop
the glutens, but you can skip it and just throw everything in at once if you're
short on time.

Add the salt and sourdough starter, then sprinkle over the remaining water.
Use your fingers to poke the starter into the dough. The dough should
already feel quite different – more elastic and silky. Keep working the dough
for 1–2 minutes, to mix through the salt and starter, and ensure that all the
flour is incorporated. Form the dough into a smooth ball in the bowl, then
cover again and leave for another 30 minutes.

Once the potatoes are ready, carefully slice them open and scoop the flesh
into a bowl. Add the rosemary, olive oil, honey or maple syrup and a pinch
of salt and pepper, and toss to combine. Set aside to cool for 10 minutes. →

Add the cooled potato mixture to the dough, stretching and folding it over itself a number of times to evenly disperse and incorporate the potato mixture. The dough now needs to undergo its fermentation. You can leave it covered in a warm place for 4–8 hours (depending on how warm it is), until the dough has risen visibly with bubbles on the surface, and it looks relaxed, silky and stretchy. Alternatively, if you'll be around the house anyway, leave the dough for just 2–3 hours and perform 4–5 'stretch and folds' every 30–45 minutes. To do this, using wet hands, simply pull up one corner of the dough to stretch it out, then fold it gently over itself. I usually go with the first option because it's easier to fit in around other things, unless I'm keen to bake the bread the same day, in which case I want to speed up the process as much as possible.

Once your dough has undergone its 'bulk ferment' you should see little bubbles on the surface and the dough should look relaxed, feel pliable and smooth and bounce back slowly when gently pressed. Turn the dough out onto a lightly floured work surface and divide in half. Dust your hands with a little flour, then, working with one piece of dough at a time, gently pick it up and fold over the corners to form a rough ball. Flip the ball over so that the smooth side is facing you, and use both hands to rotate the ball in one direction to shape it into a neater, tighter 'loaf'. As you do this you'll feel the dough becoming a little firmer, as if it's building some tension and strength. Carefully transfer each loaf, smooth side down, to a round bowl lined with a tea towel that fits it snugly, or a floured banneton if you have one. Dust with a little more flour, ensuring that the sides are floured. Cover and place in the fridge for at least 4 hours, but ideally overnight.

Preheat the oven to its maximum temperature. Place the cooking vessel in which you'll cook the bread – ideally a large flameproof casserole dish (Dutch oven), but any large, lidded pan will do (you could also use a deep baking dish and create a make-shift lid from foil) – inside the oven.

Gently tip one loaf onto a piece of baking paper. Use a sharp knife to deeply score the top of the loaf, down one side, so that it knows where to expand as it cooks. Carefully transfer the loaf to the hot dish, then quickly cover and return to the oven. Bake for 20 minutes, then remove the lid and reduce the temperature to 200°C (400°F) fan-forced. Drizzle the loaf with a little extra honey or maple syrup and flaky salt, if you like, and bake for a further 25 minutes, until the bread is deep brown and sounds hollow when tapped.

Cool the bread in the dish, or on a wire rack for at least an hour or so. It's tempting to slice it up immediately, but this will give you a weird sticky texture and ruin all your hard work – so be patient. While you wait, cook the second loaf.

Serve fresh and warm with salted butter or olive oil. →

Yeast method

Follow the instructions on page 235 to cook and prepare the potatoes.

Combine the warm water and instant dried yeast in a large bowl and set aside for 5–10 minutes, until frothy. Add the flours and salt, and mix well with a fork to form a shaggy dough. Cover and set aside to rest for 20–30 minutes.

Lightly knead the dough on a floured work surface for 3–5 minutes, until elastic and smooth, trying to limit the amount of flour you work into it as you go. This can also be done using a stand mixer with the dough hook attached. Return the dough to the bowl, cover with a damp tea towel and set aside to rise in a warm spot for 45 minutes–1½ hours, until doubled in size. Alternatively, place the covered dough in the fridge for 8–24 hours.

Add the cooled potato mixture to the dough, stretching and folding it over itself a number of times to evenly disperse and incorporate the potato mixture. Divide the dough in half, then fold and shape each piece of dough into two balls. Transfer each to a lightly oiled bowl or a floured banneton. Cover and rest for 20–60 minutes at room temperature, or for 6–8 hours in the fridge, until doubled in size again.

Continue with the sourdough method on page 236, to cook the bread.

<u>My top sourdough tips</u>

Don't bother creating a sourdough starter from scratch. It takes up to 10 days, and the odds that you'll lose interest (and waste SO much flour) are high. Instead, ask around your networks and grab some off a mate. If you live in Meanjin, message me and come and pick some up! I guarantee you that someone you know will have a jar of it in the fridge, even if they don't use it much. I got mine two years ago from my friend Anna, who got it from their neighbour who had been keeping it alive for many years.

Feed your starter with a 50/50 mix of white bread flour and rye (or wholemeal flour if you can't find rye) for best results. There's something about rye flour that seems to be more foolproof and results in a better rise.

You can always test if a starter is ready by putting a tiny pinch into a cup of water. If it floats, it's good to go. If it doesn't, your starter either needs 'feeding' or, if you've fed it recently, needs more time to rise.

Unless you're baking bread every single day, keep your starter in the fridge (especially if you live in a hot climate). I used to keep my starter on the kitchen bench and mess around feeding it every day, but it just isn't worth it, especially if you're only baking bread once or twice a week. Every time you feed your starter let it just about double at room temperature, then put it in the fridge. I use it straight from the fridge to make bread, then feed it, let it rise and return it for next time. Anyone who tells you that you need to feed your starter two or even three times before baking is lying! The fridge is your friend, and doing it this way will also ensure you basically never throw out any starter, saving you a shitload of cash for flour.

I like using a mix of flours in the dough, specifically spelt flour, which makes the bread super stretchy and delicious. You can absolutely use all white bread flour; just add a little extra water (10–20 ml/⅓ fl oz–¾ fl oz per loaf).

Sourdough dough is much stickier than other bread doughs you might be used to. Don't be afraid! This is what makes an incredible, chewy loaf. Always use wet hands to stretch and mix your dough, it makes it so much easier to handle.

Adjust your ferment time based on the temperature and humidity of where you live. You'll get a feel for this, but basically if it's cold you might need to leave the dough longer, and when it's warm the yeasts will activate quicker and you don't want to 'over-prove' the dough. Basically, in the peak of summer don't leave the dough on your kitchen bench for more than 6–8 hours max, but in winter an overnight fermentation is fine.

You can also speed up each process, including the bulk fermentation and the rising of your sourdough starter. Put a hot water bottle or a couple of cups of boiling water in an esky or your microwave and add your starter or dough. A very low oven (30–40°C/85–105°F) can also be utilised, but creating a steam room for your dough is even better. The same goes for slowing things down – you can slow the ferment at any point by putting the dough in the fridge.

Once your bread is shaped, it can rest in the fridge for up to 4 or 5 days. So if you want freshly baked bread a few times a week, and want to save time actually making the dough, make multiple loaves at once, then just pull them out for baking when you're ready for them.

You don't need a fancy bread blade to score the dough like all the videos online will tell you; just use your sharpest knife or even a small serrated knife. When you score the dough, ensure you cut deeply or it might rise strangely.

The most common way I turn out an inferior loaf is by losing patience at the cook stage and putting my bread in the oven before it is hot enough. Don't be like me. Be patient, the ideal time to get it into the dish is when you accidentally forget about it for a while, and it's absolutely scorching. ✳

Spanish potato & leek tortilla with easy tomato chutney

Serves 4–6 · Gluten Free

500–600 g (1 lb 2 oz–1 lb 5 oz) waxy potatoes, peeled and chopped into 1 cm (½ in) cubes

125 ml (½ cup) vegetable oil (or another neutral oil)

1 leek, white and pale green part, quartered lengthways, then sliced into 1 cm (½ in) pieces

1 tsp dried or fresh thyme

1 heaped tsp dijon mustard

salt and pepper

8 eggs

125 g (½ cup) sour cream

100 g (3½ oz) soft goat's cheese

basil leaves and nasturtium flowers, to serve (optional)

Easy tomato chutney

1 tbsp olive oil

½ onion, diced

2 garlic cloves, minced

500 g (1 lb 2 oz) tomatoes, roughly chopped

1 tsp smoky paprika

1 tsp cumin seeds

½ tsp salt

1–2 tbsp brown sugar, to taste

1 tbsp red wine vinegar

This tortilla is spectacularly simple, with very few ingredients. The flavour is all in the potatoes and leeks, which are cooked slow and low confit-style in oil. If you have some leftover boiled potatoes, this is a great way to use them. I love eating this tortilla alongside this easy tomato chutney, which isn't too sweet or sticky, meaning you can really load it on. Serve with a big green salad for a satisfying and easy dinner, or as is for a lovely brunch.

Place the potato in a saucepan and cover with cold water and a sprinkle of salt. Bring to the boil over medium heat and cook for 5–6 minutes, until just starting to soften. Drain and set aside to cool a little.

To make the tomato chutney, heat the olive oil, onion and garlic in a saucepan over medium–low heat. Stir gently and cook for 5 minutes or until the onion is translucent, then add the tomato, paprika, cumin seeds, salt, brown sugar and 170 ml (⅔ cup) of water. Bring the mixture to the boil, then reduce the heat to a simmer and cook for 30–40 minutes, mashing the tomato gently with a spoon as it begins to soften and break down. Once the chutney has thickened, add the vinegar and stir well. Taste and adjust the seasoning and sugar to your taste. Set aside to cool.

Preheat the oven to 180°C (350°F) fan-forced.

Meanwhile, heat the vegetable oil in an ovenproof frying pan over medium heat until hot. Reduce the heat to low and carefully add the potato and leek. Cook, stirring every 5 minutes, for about 20 minutes, until the leek has browned considerably and the potato is soft. If the potatoes and leek haven't reached this stage, increase the heat slightly and continue cooking for a little longer. Once ready, add the thyme and mustard, along with a generous pinch of salt and pepper, and stir through to combine. Taste and make sure it's really well seasoned.

Whisk the eggs, sour cream and another pinch of salt and pepper in a bowl, until well combined. Carefully pour the mixture into the pan and gently stir through the vegetables. Transfer the pan to the oven and cook for 10–15 minutes, until the egg has puffed up and is just set. Remove from the oven and spoon over the soft goat's cheese. Serve hot or at room temperature, with a generous tablespoon or two of tomato chutney and a few basil leaves and nasturtium flowers, if you like. *

Vanilla-glazed doughnuts (with secret potato)

Makes 12–14 large doughnuts · Vegan

300 g (10½ oz) potatoes, peeled and quartered

1 heaped tsp instant dried yeast

80 ml (⅓ cup) warm water

250 ml (1 cup) milk of your choice

juice of ½ lemon (about 1 tbsp)

1 tsp vanilla essence

1 tsp salt

95 g (½ cup) brown sugar

525 g (3½ cups) plain (all-purpose) flour, plus extra for dusting

vegetable oil (or another neutral oil), for shallow-frying

Vanilla glaze

60 ml (¼ cup) plant-based milk

¼ tsp salt

½ tsp vanilla essence

280 g (2¼ cups) icing (confectioners') sugar

Swaps

Brown sugar – caster (superfine) sugar

Plant-based milk and lemon juice – buttermilk

These doughnuts were an experiment that went very right. They make a fun lazy-Sunday project when you feel like baking and putting in a little effort, and are great to take along to a party or picnic. Especially so because you likely already have everything you need to make them in your pantry. Make them smaller (and reduce the cooking time a little) for a more reasonable-sized snack and you'll easily get 20 doughnuts from this batch. The potato helps provide moisture and chewiness, and gives the dough a little more depth. I get the best results by passing the soft-boiled potato through a potato ricer, but grating it finely works too – just take care not to overwork the potato or the dough.

Place the potato in a small saucepan and cover with cold water. Bring to the boil and cook for 20–25 minutes, until a fork slips easily into the potato. Drain and run under cold water to cool quickly. Using a potato ricer or a fine grater, shred the soft potato, taking care not to overmix or overwork it too much or you'll end up with a starchy glue. Transfer the potato to a mixing bowl.

Whisk the yeast and warm water together in a small bowl and set aside for 10 minutes or until foamy.

Meanwhile, whisk the milk and lemon juice together in a jug and leave to stand for a couple of minutes, until it thickens and curdles like buttermilk. Pour the mixture into the bowl with the potato and add the vanilla, salt and brown sugar. Gently stir the mixture a few times, until just combined. Add the yeasted water and gently mix again. Finally, add the flour and use your hands or a spatula to fold and gently stir the dough and bring it together. There's no need to knead this dough, but you do want to ensure all the flour is incorporated with no remaining white streaks. Cover the dough and leave it to rise in a warm place for 45–60 minutes, until doubled in size.

Dust a work surface with flour, then scoop a 2 tablespoon portion of dough (or smaller if you want to make more doughnuts), dust with a little flour and work into a smooth, round ball by pressing and folding the dough onto itself to form one smooth side. Use your finger to poke a hole in the middle of the dough round and gently stretch the hole to form a doughnut ring. I do this by swivelling the dough around my finger in a circular motion. Repeat until you've formed all the doughnuts. Set aside on a sheet of baking paper.

Half-fill a frying pan with vegetable oil and heat over medium heat. Test if the oil is hot enough with a tiny scrap of dough; if it sizzles straight away the oil is ready. Working in small batches, add the doughnuts to the oil and cook for 1 minute, then flip and cook the other side for another minute or until deep golden brown. If you find they're browning too quickly, reduce the heat a little or you'll risk burning the outsides and not cooking them all the way through. Gently transfer the doughnuts to a wire rack with paper towel underneath to drain.

As the doughnuts cool, prepare the glaze by mixing the plant-based milk, salt and vanilla together in a small bowl. Add most of the icing sugar and mix well to form a thick glaze, taking care to press out any icing sugar lumps. Depending on the milk you've used, add the remaining icing sugar, or hold back if you think it's thick enough. You want the glaze thin enough to coat the doughnuts, but thick enough that it won't all drip off.

Once the doughnuts have cooled and are no longer piping hot (a little warm is okay), dunk them generously in the glaze, then return to the wire rack, glazed side up. Eat fresh, though they'll keep okay for a day or two in an airtight container. ✳

Pumpkin

Recipes

A whopping big pumpkin (winter squash) can go such
a long way, feeding the masses for days in sweet and savoury
dishes. They're so damn easy to grow yourself, too, if you
have some space in the garden to completely let them take
over. When cooking pumpkin, take the care and time to do it
right – there's not much worse than stringy, or undercooked
pumpkin. Whenever I crack open a whole pumpkin I tend to
roast the whole thing in wedges in a hot oven until soft and
a little caramelised. Roasted pumpkin can be kept in the fridge
for up to a week, or frozen for months. Many of the recipes in
this chapter were conceived with pumpkin prepared this way,
then mashed and incorporated into a meal or dish later.

With Marilena, Rae, Jay, Cornelius, Lachlan, Tiana and Kat

Describe your household

The intention for this house was to turn Marilena's Italian grandparents' villa into a queer, artist commune ... And it has become that and so much more. Their Nono (Orazio Mamarella) and Nina (Maria Mamarella) found refuge in Australia just after World War II. Thirty years later Orazio paid homage to his homeland by building this astonishing home for Nina, Marilena's mum (Marilena Maria Mamarella) and her four sisters. It is a rare and special gift that we now get to share it and, like those before us, fill it with food, wine and love. There are seven of us who live among the four floors. There is Lachlan, tattoo artist and record slinger; Jay, film-maker; Cornelius, artist and designer; Rae, film-maker and lawyer; Tiana, conceptual artist and arts worker; Kat, fashion designer and tailor; and Marilena, amateur publisher, designer and part-time caterer.

Do you share food as a household?

All the time! We all live for food and each other's company. Sometimes we just need to eat chocolate in bed and watch *X Files*, though. Which is also respected. Our favourite thing to make together is pasta. We love rolling pici while fresh tomato sugo simmers on the stove. I can't recommend making pici with a big group of mates enough! Eating is so much more special when you all get to play chef beforehand. It's so cheap and simple too – all you need is water, oil and flour.

What do you love about living in a share house?

It is the most special way to occupy space. Friends and strangers become family in no time. There is lots to learn and gain from sharing intimate space. Self-awareness, creativity, deep connection, maintenance and support just to name a few. Like any fragile ecosystem, the more work, love and care you give the more you receive. When someone is down there is someone to pick them up with a hug or food or a long chat.

What gives you hope for a better world?

If we have learned anything from share-housing it is that sharing is a luxury, not a compromise. If this were a universal notion we might treat non-humans, the land, each other and ourselves better. Hope and joy can be found in deep respect for what is right here, like our friend Pudge, a pigeon who comes to see us every afternoon. *

Pumpkin scones with whipped butter

Makes 9–12

75 g (2¾ oz) very cold salted butter, grated or chopped into small pieces

100 g (1 cup) grated vintage cheddar, plus extra handful for sprinkling

450 g (3 cups) self-raising flour, plus extra for dusting

½ tsp salt

½ tsp white pepper

250 g (9 oz) roasted pumpkin (winter squash) (from 375 g/13 oz raw), mashed until smooth

185 ml (¾ cup) buttermilk (make your own buttermilk by stirring 2 tsp of lemon juice into milk and letting it stand for a couple of minutes)

40 g (1½ oz) pumpkin seeds (pepitas)

handful of grated parmesan

chutney or hot sauce, to serve

Whipped butter

150 g (5½ oz) salted butter, at room temperature

2 tbsp cream or milk

generous pinch of flaky sea salt

Swaps

Vegan – butter: olive oil; buttermilk: oat milk mixed with 2 tsp of lemon juice; cheese: vegan cheese

Leftover roasted pumpkin? Chuck it in some scones and enjoy snack heaven. Laced with sharp cheddar and topped with crunchy pumpkin seeds, these simple scones are easy to make but so satisfying to eat. In fact, somehow, of all the recipes that housemates and friends have taste-tested for this book, these scones seem to be everyone's favourite. I'm not sure I'd go that far, but they definitely strike a chord, especially when served with whipped butter and a little dash of hot sauce.

Preheat the oven to 200°C (400°F) fan-forced. Line a baking tray with baking paper.

Place the butter, cheddar, flour, salt and pepper in a mixing bowl and use your fingers to rub the butter into the flour to create a chunky breadcrumb-like mix. Don't worry about leaving some substantial chunks of butter or cheese unmixed. Add the pumpkin and buttermilk and use a wooden spoon to bring the mixture together to form a thick, slightly sticky dough.

Working quickly, dust your hands with flour, then divide the dough into 9–12 balls and place them on the baking tray evenly spaced apart. Press a generous pinch of the pumpkin seeds into the top of each piece of dough, then scatter over the extra cheddar and the parmesan. Don't worry if the toppings don't all stay on the scones, the bits that fall off will cook and crisp around the scones.

Bake for 20–25 minutes, until the scones have risen and the cheese is golden.

Meanwhile, place the butter and cream or milk in a small bowl and use electric beaters to whip the mixture until it is smooth and light, taking care not to overmix. Sprinkle over the flaky sea salt. Keep the butter at room temperature before serving that day, then store any leftovers in the fridge for up to 1 week.

Serve the warm scones with the whipped butter and some chutney or a swig of hot sauce. *

Thai-style pumpkin soup with chilli lentils

Serves 4–6 · Vegan · Gluten Free

1 kg (2 lb 3 oz) pumpkin (winter squash), chopped into big chunks

2 carrots, roughly chopped

1 large onion, roughly chopped

5 garlic cloves, peeled

60 ml (¼ cup) olive oil

salt and pepper

30 g (1 oz) ginger, peeled and grated or finely chopped

60 g (¼ cup) Thai yellow curry paste

500–750 ml (2–3 cups) vegetable stock

400 ml (13½ fl oz) tin coconut cream

2 tbsp vegan fish sauce

fresh herbs, to serve

1 long red chilli, chopped, to serve (optional)

flatbread or toast, to serve

Chilli lentils

2 x 400 g (14 oz) tins brown lentils, rinsed and drained

2 tbsp olive oil

salt and pepper

1 tbsp sriracha or chilli sauce of your choice

Swaps

Carrots – extra onion, 1 small sweet potato or regular potato

Pumpkin (winter squash) – sweet potato

Roasting veggies is my favourite way to make vegetable soup. Not only does the roasting impart a lovely flavour, it's also very quick and easy, meaning all that's left to do is add liquid, bring to the boil and blend before serving. Using a premade curry paste makes this particular soup very easy, but you could definitely substitute a homemade curry paste of any variety. Roasted, crispy chilli lentils add protein and texture, but oven-roasted chickpeas or cannellini beans would be delicious too.

Preheat the oven to 200°C (400°F) fan-forced. Line a large baking tray with baking paper and add the pumpkin, carrot, onion and garlic. Drizzle with the olive oil and sprinkle over some salt and pepper. Bake for 30–35 minutes, until the vegetables are soft and beginning to brown.

Meanwhile, spread the drained lentils across a clean tea towel, to absorb some of the excess liquid. Leave them to dry while the vegetables are roasting. You can skip this step if using a bulkier legume, such as chickpeas (garbanzo beans).

Mix the ginger, curry paste and 2 tablespoons of water together in a small bowl. Remove the vegetables from the oven and turn them over, then drizzle the curry paste mixture over the top and toss to coat. Return to the oven and bake for another 8–10 minutes, watching closely to ensure that the paste doesn't start to burn.

Transfer the lentils to a large baking tray, drizzle over the olive oil, season with a pinch of salt and pepper and add the chilli sauce. Use your hands to toss the lentils until completely coated in the oil mixture, then spread them across the tray in an even layer.

Remove the vegetables from the oven and increase the temperature to 250°C (480°F) fan-forced. Bake the lentils for 10 minutes, then remove from the oven to toss them well. Bake for a further 10 minutes or until crisp, keeping a close eye on them to ensure that they don't burn.

Meanwhile, transfer the roasted vegetables to a saucepan and set over medium heat. Add 500 ml (2 cups) of the vegetable stock and most of the coconut cream. Bring the mixture to the boil, adding the remaining stock if you prefer a thinner soup.

Use a stick blender to blend the mixture to a silky, smooth soup. Stir in the fish sauce, then taste and adjust the seasoning if necessary. Divide the soup among bowls and top with a few fresh herbs, the chilli (if using) and the crispy lentils. Drizzle over the remaining coconut cream and serve with flatbread or toast on the side.

Leftover soup will keep in the fridge for up to 1 week. Store any leftover lentils in an airtight container in the fridge – they make a great addition to salads and other meals. *

Pumpkin pesto agnolotti

Serves 4–6

400 g (2⅔ cups) 00 flour, plus extra
for dusting

4 eggs

2 tbsp olive oil

75 g (2¾ oz) salted butter

125 ml (½ cup) pouring cream

Basil pesto

85 g (⅔ cup) sunflower seeds

100 g (1 cup) grated parmesan, plus
extra to serve

juice of 1 lemon (about 1 tbsp), plus
extra if needed

1–2 garlic cloves, peeled

large bunch of basil, leaves picked

60 ml (¼ cup) olive oil, plus extra for
drizzling

salt and pepper

Pumpkin filling

1 egg

¼ tsp nutmeg (ideally freshly grated)

150 g (5½ oz) firm ricotta

250 g (9 oz) roasted pumpkin (winter
squash) (from 375 g/13 oz raw)

2 tbsp basil pesto (see above)

*I don't make much filled pasta, as I often find the fillings dry and boring.
But the inside of these agnolotti is super soft and silky, bursting out of
the pasta when you take a bite and marrying beautifully with the sauce.
I love using sunflower seeds in pesto because you can include a really large
whack of them (for dirt cheap), which gives the pesto a bit more substance
and protein, and when blended provides a delicious creamy nuttiness.
When made completely from scratch, this recipe is a bit of a labour of love
but there are so many cheats to simplify it and cut corners, so it's really
up to you to choose your own adventure. Use leftover roasted pumpkin,
replace the homemade pasta dough with premade fresh lasagne sheets
and/or sub out the homemade pesto for your favourite jarred stuff.*

Tip the flour onto a clean work surface or into a large bowl. Create a large well
in the centre and crack in the eggs. Using a fork, gently whisk the egg, gradually
bringing in the flour from the sides to create a thicker and thicker paste. Once
the mixture resembles a rough dough, add the olive oil, then knead with your
hands for 5–8 minutes, until smooth and elastic. Cover the dough with a clean
tea towel or plastic wrap and transfer to the fridge to rest.

To make the basil pesto, blitz the sunflower seeds, parmesan, lemon juice,
1 garlic clove and 60 ml (¼ cup) of water in a food processor or blender until
smooth. Add the basil leaves and olive oil and blitz again until just combined,
adding a little extra water if necessary to get things moving. Taste and add the
remaining garlic and more lemon juice if you like, and season generously with
salt and pepper. Give the pesto a final blitz to finish, then scoop 2 tablespoons
into a bowl and transfer the rest to a separate bowl and drizzle with olive oil to
prevent it browning. Set aside until ready to serve.

To make the pumpkin filling, add the egg, nutmeg, ricotta and pumpkin to the
2 tablespoons of pesto. Mash well with a fork to form a smooth paste, then
taste and adjust the seasoning as required

Divide the dough into four or five pieces and roll out on a lightly floured work
surface to create 1 mm (1⁄16 in) thick long sheets. If using a pasta machine,
roll each piece through the machine to the sixth setting or until 1 mm (1⁄16 in)
thick. Lay the pasta sheets on a lightly floured work surface and place heaped
teaspoons of the pumpkin filling at 3–4 cm (1¼–1½ in) intervals along the
bottom half of each sheet, leaving a 1 cm (½ in) border at the base. Fold the top
half of each pasta sheet over the filling and use your fingers to seal the pasta
around the filling, creating tight pockets. Cut the pasta between each blob of
filling and press the ends together to seal, ensuring there are no air pockets.
Neaten the agnolotti using a pizza slicer or a pasta or pastry cutter. Transfer
the agnolotti to a plate or board and, if you've made them ahead of time, store
in the freezer until you're ready to cook.

Bring a large saucepan of very salty water to the boil.

Swaps

00 flour – plain (all-purpose) flour

Basil pesto – 150 g (5½ oz) store-bought pesto

Homemade pasta sheets – 375 g (13 oz) store-bought fresh lasagne sheets, using a beaten egg to help seal the agnolotti

Sunflower seeds – pumpkin seeds (pepitas), pine nuts, almonds or walnuts

Melt the butter in a frying pan over medium heat for 3–5 minutes, until it begins to brown and smell nutty. Add the cream and remaining pesto and stir until well combined. Turn off the heat.

Cook the agnolotti in the boiling water in 2–3 batches for a couple of minutes, stirring gently to ensure that they don't stick to the bottom. When the agnolotti rise to the top they're ready. Use a slotted spoon to transfer the agnolotti to the frying pan with the pesto sauce. Scoop out 125 ml (½ cup) of the starchy pasta water and pour half of it into the frying pan. Return the pan to medium heat and gently heat, moving the agnolotti around to coat them in the pesto sauce and help emulsify the pasta water. Once the sauce has thickened, divide the pasta among bowls, top with a little extra parmesan and freshly cracked black pepper, and serve. ✳

Roast pumpkin with crunchy chickpeas, peanuts & coconut cream

Serves 4–6 · Vegan · Gluten Free

1.25 kg (2 lb 12 oz) pumpkin (winter squash), cut into 2 cm (¾ in) thick slices

2 tbsp olive oil, plus extra for drizzling

salt and pepper

2 x 400 g (14 oz) tins chickpeas (garbanzo beans), rinsed and drained

1 tbsp cumin seeds

80 g (½ cup) peanuts

¼ red onion, thinly sliced

6 makrut lime leaves, very thinly shredded

large handful of Thai basil leaves

Coconut cream dressing

200 ml (7 fl oz) tinned coconut cream

2 tbsp soy sauce or tamari

2 tbsp white vinegar

1 tsp chilli sauce, plus extra to serve (optional)

salt and pepper

Swaps

Pumpkin (winter squash) – sweet potato, potato, broccoli or cauliflower

Thai basil – basil, mint or coriander (cilantro) leaves

This plate of food is a heavenly combination of textures and flavours. It was a slightly scrambled-together meal the first time I made it, but now it is one I turn to regularly. Inspired by Malaysian and Indonesian flavours, I suppose it's a bit of a deconstructed satay. The fragrant tiny slivers of lime leaf and Thai basil pair wonderfully with the silky, simple coconut cream dressing, and the lashings of roasted nuts and chickpeas provide enough substance that this feels like a complete meal. Pair with some roti and your favourite spicy condiment and call it a day.

Preheat the oven to 200°C (400°F) fan-forced.

As the oven warms, arrange the pumpkin slices on your largest baking tray, giving them as much space as possible (or spread them across two trays to avoid overlapping). Drizzle with 1 tablespoon of the olive oil and season well with salt and pepper. Place the chickpeas on a separate baking tray, drizzle with the remaining oil, season with salt and pepper and gently toss to combine.

Place the pumpkin in the oven and roast for 45 minutes or until soft and slightly charring at the edges. Add the chickpeas after 10 minutes and cook for 25 minutes, tossing them halfway through cooking. Add the cumin seeds and peanuts and toss them through the chickpeas, then return to the oven and cook for a final 10 minutes.

Meanwhile, prepare the coconut cream dressing by whisking the ingredients in a small bowl. Season to taste with salt and pepper.

Arrange the roasted pumpkin slices over a large serving plate or shallow bowl. Spoon or pour the dressing over the pumpkin, then scoop over the crispy chickpeas and peanuts. Scatter with the red onion, lime leaf and Thai basil, and finish with an extra drizzle of olive oil and a shake of chilli sauce, if you like. Serve warm or at room temperature. *

Spiced pumpkin cinnamon scrolls

Makes 16–20

435 ml (1¾ cups) warm milk

1 tsp instant dried yeast

150 g (5½ oz) unsalted butter, melted

2 tsp salt

300 g (10½ oz) roasted pumpkin (winter squash) (from 450 g/1 lb raw), mashed or blended until smooth

1 egg

95 g (½ cup) brown sugar

1 heaped tsp ground cinnamon

¼ tsp ground ginger

900 g (6 cups) plain (all-purpose) flour or bread flour (1.05 kg/7 cups if using the sourdough method), plus extra for dusting

Spiced sugar filling

200 g (7 oz) salted butter, softened

230 g (1 firmly packed cup) brown sugar

2 tbsp maple syrup

2 tsp ground cinnamon

½ tsp nutmeg (ideally freshly grated)

½ tsp ground ginger

2 tsp vanilla essence

pinch of salt

1–2 tbsp warm water

Cream-cheese icing

75 g (2¾ oz) salted butter, softened

150 g (5½ oz) cream cheese, softened

60 g (½ cup) icing (confectioners') sugar

1 tbsp maple syrup

This recipe makes a large quantity of cinnamon scrolls, because they are too good (and a little too much effort) not to share. Can you think of a better doorstep gift than a plate of warm cinnamon scrolls? Nope. Mashed or blended pumpkin adds a beautiful moisture and lovely colour, and complements the classic pumpkin-spice flavours well. If you have an active sourdough starter you could substitute 100 g (3½ oz) for the yeast, reduce the milk by a few tablespoons and leave the dough overnight in the fridge (or on your kitchen bench if the weather is cool) to ferment.

Whisk the warm milk and yeast together in a very large bowl. Set aside for 5–10 minutes for the yeast to activate.

Add the remaining ingredients except the flour to the yeast mixture and stir well to combine. Fold in the flour and bring the mixture together to form a shaggy dough. Using lightly floured hands, knead the dough for 5–10 minutes by lifting it up and pressing it onto itself, until it is stretchy and smooth. Add a little extra flour if the dough is too sticky to work with, but try to avoid adding too much as the wet dough makes for a nicer scroll. Cover the bowl with a damp tea towel and set aside to rise in a warm spot until doubled in size. This will take anywhere between 1 and 3 hours on your kitchen bench, or 12–24 hours in the fridge if you're making it a day ahead.

When the dough is almost ready, combine the filling ingredients in a bowl, adding enough warm water to create a spreadable paste. Set aside at room temperature until ready to use.

Tip the dough onto a lightly floured work surface and use your hands or a rolling pin to stretch it out to a large rectangle, about 1 cm (½ in) thick. You can do this in two batches if it's easier. With a long edge facing you, spread the filling across the surface of the dough, then gently roll it into a long log. Cut the log into 16–20 pieces, about 2 cm (¾ in) wide.

Line a large deep baking tray with baking paper and add the scrolls, spaced 5 mm (¼ in) apart so they have room to rise. Cover with a damp tea towel and set aside in a warm spot for 15–30 minutes, until slightly risen.

Meanwhile, preheat the oven to 200°C (400°F) fan-forced.

Transfer the scrolls to the oven and bake for 25–35 minutes, until risen and turning dark brown. Set aside to cool for 5–10 minutes.

To make the cream-cheese icing, use electric beaters to beat the butter and cream cheese together in a bowl until smooth and silky. Add the icing sugar, maple syrup and a pinch of salt and beat until soft and light. Set aside at room temperature until ready to use.

Once the scrolls have cooled a little, spread the icing over the top and serve. Store leftovers in an airtight container in the fridge for 3–4 days, warming them for 20 seconds in the microwave before eating. ✳

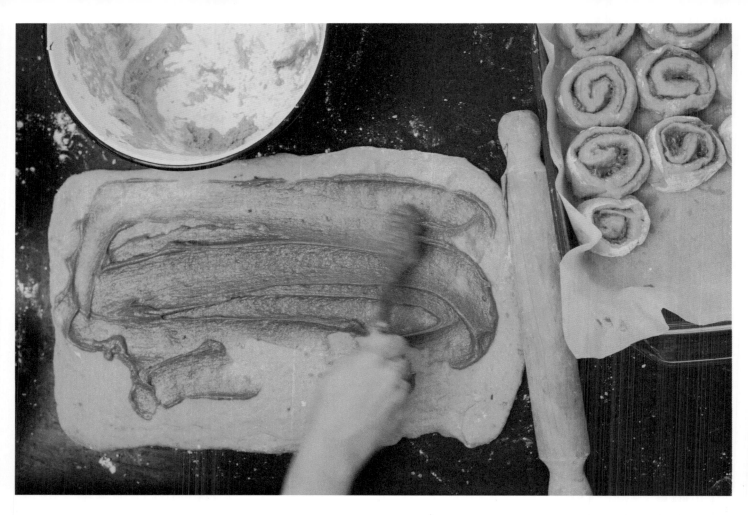

Strawberries

To be fair, it's probably a bit of a stretch to consider strawberries a cheap and easily available fruit. But for a glorious month or two of the year they are in abundant excess, and I always find myself overwhelmed with where to begin cooking with the bounty. When strawberry season hit as I was writing this book, I piled our fridge high and tested all manner of recipes – these are the crowd favourites that made the cut. All of the dishes here can be altered to include whatever berry or stone fruit is cheap and available to you, or substituted with frozen berries.

With Shannon and Hannah

Describe your household

Hannah, a graphic designer for the Queensland Greens, her very sweet dog and partner in crime, Bee, and Shannon, who owns a cute little leafy salon in West End. We've lived together for two years.

How do you navigate sharing a kitchen?

We shop at the Milton Markets together almost every weekend and take turns cooking most nights of the week. We are pretty similarly tidy people, so cleaning isn't really a problem. We tend to just clean our own mess, so if it's not your night to cook you get a complete night off from the kitchen which is so nice! We usually talk about what we want to eat for the week and take it in turns around our schedules.

What's your favourite way to cook/eat strawberries?

Any way really, but we especially love strawberry jam with fresh scones.

Who's the best cook in your house and why?

Hannah: 'I've loved baking since I was a kid and tend to stress bake (although our rental oven is not the best for baking!). We grew up on a pretty isolated farm in rural New South Wales and my mum taught me how to make a meal from almost anything you have in the pantry, or how to adjust a recipe to work with what you have – she's a great cook!'

What gives you and your housemate hope for a better world?

We both get caught up feeling like nobody cares about the same things that we do. But the more you talk to other people, and try to do good work, the more you realise there are really great people who do give a fuck, who are also fighting for a better world. ✳

Strawberry, feta & mint salad

Serves 4–6 as a side · Gluten Free

250 g (9 oz) strawberries, hulled and sliced in half or thirds

2 Lebanese cucumbers, halved lengthways and sliced into chunky half moons

150 g (5½ oz) feta, cubed

3 radishes, halved and thinly sliced

handful of mint leaves, plus extra to serve

Herb oil dressing

2 handfuls of mint leaves

2 handfuls of basil leaves

60 ml (¼ cup) olive oil

salt and pepper

1 tbsp white wine vinegar

Swaps

Vegan – feta: vegan feta or salted avocado cubes

Feta – goat's cheese or grilled haloumi

This salad was conceived on a climate-anxiety-inducing sweltering spring day when cooking was unfathomable. It's super moreish and fresh. Strawberries pair so incredibly here with creamy, salty feta and loads of refreshing cucumber and radish. A zingy herb oil brings it all together and firmly establishes the savouriness of the salad. I think it'll win over even the most sceptical in the 'no fruits in savoury dishes' camp.

To make the herb oil dressing, bring a small saucepan of water to a slow boil. Blanch the herb leaves for 5–10 seconds, then swiftly drain and transfer to a bowl of icy-cold water, or run under a cold tap until completely cool. Transfer the wilted leaves to a blender along with the remaining dressing ingredients. Whiz together, adding a splash of water if necessary to get things moving and blend until well combined. Taste and ensure that there's some saltiness and tartness coming through, adding extra salt and pepper, to your taste.

Just before serving, combine the salad ingredients in a serving dish or shallow bowl. Drizzle over the dressing and scatter with extra mint leaves. Serve immediately. ✳

Strawberry & dark chocolate tart

Serves 8–10

200 g (7 oz) chocolate ripple biscuits (plain chocolate cookies) (the rest of the packet is for the chef to snack on)

100 g (3½ oz) salted butter, melted

500 g (1 lb 2 oz) strawberries, hulled and sliced

1 tbsp caster (superfine) sugar

300 g (10½ oz) double-thickened (dollop) cream

edible dried flowers or mint leaves, to serve (optional)

Custard

310 ml (1¼ cups) milk

4 egg yolks

1½ tsp vanilla essence

115 g (½ cup) caster (superfine) sugar

25 g (1 oz) cornflour (corn starch)

pinch of salt

150 g (5½ oz) dark chocolate (at least 70% cocoa solids), chopped

Swaps

Gluten free – ripple biscuits: gluten-free chocolate biscuits (cookies)

Ripple biscuits – another chocolate biscuit

Strawberries – another berry, roasted rhubarb, poached pear or sliced figs

My memory of birthdays as a kid just about always involved a chocolate cake with a tub of double-thickened cream and a punnet of lightly sugared strawberries. It's such a perfectly classic flavour combination that I can never stray far from. Though this tart is a little more complex than those birthday cakes, the flavours hold true and it's so delicious without being sickeningly rich or sweet. If you've never made a set custard before, this is a perfect recipe to try your hand – it's pretty simple and immensely satisfying when you pull it out of the fridge, slice into it and see how perfectly your custard has set. I've topped the tart with a sprinkle of edible dried flowers, but a few mint leaves would be lovely too.

Preheat the oven to 200°C (400°F) fan-forced.

Blitz the biscuits in a food processor to form a fine crumb. Add the melted butter and blitz again to form a thick paste. If you don't have a food processor you can bash the biscuits under a clean tea towel with a rolling pin, but it'll take a while. It's important that the crumb is fine so you can press it into the side of the tart tin.

Transfer the crumb mixture to a 25 cm (10 in) tart tin with a removable base or a small springform cake tin if that's what you have. Use wet hands to press the mixture into the base of the tin and 2 cm (¾ in) up the side. Take your time doing this, to form an even base, keeping your hands wet to prevent the mixture peeling away as you work. The tart shell will shrink a little as it cooks, so take care to press the mixture firmly into the side of the tin, gently building height as you go. Carefully transfer to the oven and bake for about 10 minutes, then set aside to cool completely. The butter will re-melt in the oven and then harden as it cools, so don't freak out that it doesn't look cooked.

Meanwhile, to prepare the custard, heat the milk in a small saucepan over medium–low heat until it just starts to simmer, then turn off the heat. Whisk the egg yolks, vanilla, sugar, cornflour and salt in a large bowl to form a glossy paste, then very slowly dribble in the piping-hot milk while whisking constantly. The hot milk will gently cook the egg yolks and the mixture will look bubbly and frothy.

Pour the mixture into the saucepan and return to a very low heat, whisking constantly. Gently warm the custard for 5–8 minutes, until it starts to thicken. At this stage, add the chocolate and turn off the heat, then whisk until the chocolate has completely melted. You should be left with a silky custard.

Once the tart shell has completely cooled and hardened, pour the custard over the top, spreading with a spatula to evenly fill the shell. Set aside in the fridge for about 2 hours, until the custard has set.

Just before you're ready to serve, toss the strawberries with the sugar in a bowl. Spread the cream over the top of the tart and spoon over the sugared strawberries. Finish with edible dried flowers or mint leaves, if you like. ✳

No-churn strawberries & cream ice cream

Serves 8–10 · Gluten Free

1 kg (2 lb 3 oz) strawberries, hulled and halved

400 ml (13½ fl oz) thickened (double/heavy) cream

395 g (14 oz) tin condensed milk

300 g (10½ oz) soft ricotta

2 tsp vanilla essence

To serve (optional)

extra chopped berries of your choice

whipped cream

edible flowers

waffle cones

Swaps

Strawberries – other berries

Ice cream is undoubtedly my favourite dessert but not one I make all that much, because until recently I couldn't justify the space an ice-cream churner takes up in cramped share-house kitchens. The combination of ingredients in this recipe means you can get creamy, light ice cream without needing one. There's a big punch of strawberry flavour, but the ricotta lightens it up beautifully. If you'd like it less sweet, just use less condensed milk. Although expensive for much of the year, during that sweet month or two when strawberries are piled high at every market and supermarket, this is a fun and different way to use a heap of them. You could also absolutely use frozen berries in place of fresh.

Place the strawberries in a small saucepan with a splash of water and set over medium–low heat. Cook for 7–8 minutes, until the strawberries start to break down and become soft and jammy. Continue to cook, stirring frequently to prevent them from sticking to the base of the pan, for 5 minutes or until they've completely collapsed and reduced. This step reduces the water content in the strawberries, ensuring that you don't end up with icy ice cream. Mash the berries with a potato masher or fork to make a relatively smooth sauce, then set aside to cool to lukewarm or room temperature.

Pour the cream into a large bowl and whisk or whip it until thick, with soft peaks. Add the condensed milk, ricotta and vanilla and whisk again until combined. Pour in the strawberry sauce and whisk again until the mixture is evenly pink with no white spots.

Transfer the mixture to a baking dish that fits in your freezer (or you can just keep it in the bowl) and freeze for 3–6 hours, stirring it around a little after 2 hours to help it set evenly. Alternatively, freeze overnight.

Serve the ice cream with chopped strawberries, whipped cream and edible flowers in bowls or waffle cones. Store any remaining ice cream in an airtight container in the freezer for up to 1 week. Allow the ice cream to sit at room temperature for 15 minutes before serving. ✳

Silky strawberry cheesecake

Serves 12–16

250 g (9 oz) salted butter biscuits (cookies) (I use Digestives)

80 g (½ cup) roasted unsalted peanuts, chopped

30 g (½ cup) shredded coconut

½ tsp ground cinnamon

½ tsp salt

175 g (6 oz) salted butter, melted

halved strawberries, to serve

Strawberry topping

500 g (1 lb 2 oz) strawberries, hulled

55 g (¼ cup) caster (superfine) sugar

2 tbsp freshly squeezed lemon juice

2 tbsp cornflour (corn starch)

Cheesecake filling

300 ml (10 fl oz) thickened (double/heavy) cream

500 g (1 lb 2 oz) cream cheese, softened

125 g (½ cup) sour cream

145 g (⅔ cup) caster (superfine) sugar

3 tbsp icing (confectioners') sugar

pinch of salt

1 tsp freshly squeezed lemon juice

1 tsp vanilla essence

Most of my formative memories are very squarely anchored by things I ate, including a piece of cheesecake from a cosy cafe in Copenhagen, where I spent the better part of a year during uni. A very new friend and I ducked into a coffee shop to escape the blistering cold wind and bought a piece to share, mostly because it cost way less than a coffee. This piece of cheesecake was a significant bonding experience. It was easily the most delicious one either of us had ever eaten, with the most heavenly smooth creamy inside, and a crust that made up a third of the overall slice and loaded with unexpected crunchy bits. Of course, over the coming months we made frequent visits to 'the cheesecake shop', taking everyone we met to experience the simple perfection of the slice. I've since searched for a cheesecake that might compare, but everything comes short, so this recipe is my attempt to recreate it. I love making this in a large sheet pan and slicing up squares as you need it. Although you could theoretically make it in the morning to eat that night, it does improve after a night in the fridge.

Preheat the oven to 180°C (350°F) fan-forced. Line a large sheet pan (about 35 cm x 25 cm/14 in x 10 in) with baking paper.

Pulse the biscuits, peanuts, coconut, cinnamon and salt in a food processor until roughly chopped, ideally keeping some bits more chunky as this creates a nice texture. If you don't have a food processor you can bash the biscuits with a mallet or potato masher in a bag until they're mostly crushed up, then combine with the peanuts (chopped up a bit), coconut, cinnamon and salt in a bowl. Add the melted butter and pulse again (or stir well) to combine.

Using wet hands, press the biscuit base into the base of the pan, ensuring that you press it right into the corners. Transfer to the oven and bake for 10–15 minutes, until the base smells biscuity and looks golden. Remove from the oven and set aside to cool completely. You can speed this up by putting the pan (once cool enough to touch) in the fridge or freezer.

Next, blitz the strawberry topping ingredients in a food processor or blender until smooth, adding a splash or two of water if necessary to get everything moving. Transfer to a saucepan and place over medium heat. Bring the mixture to a slow simmer and cook, stirring frequently to prevent it from sticking to the base of the pan, for 10 minutes or until thickened and dark red. Remove from the heat and set aside to cool completely (again, you can transfer it to a bowl in the fridge or freezer to speed things up).

Swaps

Gluten free – salted butter biscuits (cookies): similar gluten-free biscuits

Peanuts – crunchy peanut butter

Shredded coconut – desiccated coconut or almond/hazelnut meal

To make the cheesecake filling, use a whisk or electric beaters to slowly whip the cream in a bowl until stiff peaks form. In a separate large bowl, whisk or beat the cream cheese until smooth and light (warm the cream cheese a little in the microwave first if it's too cold). Add the remaining filling ingredients and beat for 2–3 minutes, until thick silky ripples follow the beaters and the mixture looks super glossy. Gently fold in the whipped cream, being careful not to beat out the air. Continue folding the mixture until the cream is completely incorporated. Spread the filling over the cooled biscuit base, using a rubber spatula to smooth it out evenly. Gently pour or spoon over the cooled strawberry topping and spread to cover evenly.

Transfer the cheesecake to the fridge to set for at least 6 hours, but ideally 12–24 hours. Cut the cheesecake into small squares and top with halved strawberries. Store any leftovers in the fridge for 4–5 days, or in the freezer for up to 3 months. ✳

Tomato

If there was one fruit or vegetable I couldn't live without, it would probably be tomatoes. Cooked into a flavourful pasta or pizza sauce, or simply blistered in the oven with plenty of seasoning, tomatoes are powerhouses. In the summer months, when they're plump, juicy and perfectly sweet, I like them best sliced on homemade bread with some seasoning, olive oil and a bit of fresh basil from the garden. They inspire plenty of more complex meals too, and I was hard-pressed narrowing these recipes down for this book. Some of these recipes rely on fresh tomatoes, but for others feel free to substitute tinned tomatoes in the cooler months.

With James, Thomas and Al

Describe your household

Our household follows a long tradition of queer share houses on Browning Street in West End, and is currently occupied by Thomas, James and Al.

Al is a hard-working activist who always seems to find new and creative ways to fight against injustice in a variety of spaces, such as Refugee Solidarity Meanjin and Growing Forward.

James works in digital marketing and is constantly expanding his creative universe into new spaces, already having made his mark in the drag scene as The Silver Stone, and the literary scene with his publication, *PASTEL*.

Thomas (aka DJ Sweaty Baby) is a bit of a 'slashie': he's an arts worker/DJ/ creative producer, and was formerly even a labour lawyer, but he devotes most of his time to planning the next grand iteration of his queer dance party, Shandy.

Who's the best cook in your house and why?

James and Al cook often and it's a toss-up as to who's the best chef. James is always trying something new, but Al makes great vegan food and is very good at keeping things tidy. Thomas doesn't cook too much, but when he can find the motivation, he'll end up spending hours in the kitchen cooking up an amazing feast for everyone.

What does a typical Saturday morning in your house look like?

We usually enjoy each other's company and discuss weekend plans/life while lying in bed, or have coffee and breakfast on the lawn and soak up the sun.

What's your favourite way to cook/eat tomatoes?

Al's mum makes a really good tomato chutney that everyone loves. It's been a family favourite for three generations. If tomatoes are ripe and in season, we all agree that your best bet is to buy a loaf of fresh sourdough from a local bakery and top it simply with sliced tomato, olive oil and a pinch of salt. ✳

A simple tomato salad

Serves 4–6 as a side · Vegan · Gluten Free

125 ml (½ cup) olive oil

3 tbsp rosemary leaves

5 garlic cloves, thinly sliced

1 long red chilli, thinly sliced

1 tsp flaky salt

750 g (1 lb 11 oz) mixed tomatoes, thickly sliced (or halved if using cherry tomatoes)

1 large ripe avocado, thickly sliced

cracked black pepper

This is what you should make during those glorious few weeks of the year when your (or your mate's) garden tomatoes are going wild, or saving that, they're bright, colourful and cheap to buy. This salad is very simple and only takes five minutes to prepare, but it's dressed with a flavoursome garlic and rosemary oil, which makes it really special. It was conceived as something akin to caprese, perhaps its vegan, slightly fiery, cousin. Add some extra salad leaves, basil or some thinly sliced onion if you'd like to bulk it up. It would be lovely with some cannellini beans or lentils to turn it into a light meal. But like most dishes made with in-season tomatoes, simplicity is your friend.

Heat the olive oil in a small frying pan over low heat. Once the oil is hot, add the rosemary and garlic, spreading the ingredients out so they have space to sizzle gently. Cook for 1–2 minutes, taking care not to burn the garlic, then add the chilli and cook for another minute or until the garlic is lightly golden and the rosemary is slightly shrivelled and crisp. Stir through the flaky salt, then set aside to cool for a few minutes.

Lay the tomato and avocado across a large serving plate or dish. Evenly spoon the fried garlic, rosemary and chilli over the top and drizzle with the oil. Finish the salad with some cracked pepper and an extra pinch of salt, and serve. ✳

Baked ricotta & tomatoes with crunchy seeds

Serves 6–8 as a side or starter · Gluten Free

750 g (1 lb 11 oz) firm ricotta, sliced into 2 cm (¾ in) thick wedges

1 kg (2 lb 3 oz) tomatoes (any variety), halved or quartered, depending on their size

60 ml (¼ cup) olive oil, plus extra for drizzling

1 tbsp honey

40 g (⅓ cup) sunflower seeds

2 tbsp fennel seeds

2 tbsp caraway seeds

1 tsp flaky salt

cracked black pepper

2 tbsp caramelised balsamic vinegar

2 handfuls of oregano or basil leaves

crusty bread, to serve

Swaps

Vegan – ricotta: medium or firm tofu, cut into 1 cm (½ in) thick slices and seasoned well; honey: maple syrup or brown sugar

Caraway seeds – cumin seeds or bashed coriander seeds

Sunflower seeds – pumpkin seeds (pepitas), chopped walnuts or almonds

Tomatoes – pumpkin (winter squash), fennel, red or brown onion, capsicums (bell peppers) or mushrooms

This dish makes a delicious starter or party snack, served alongside some bread and dips. I love how easy it is, and that it can be made ahead of time. As the tomatoes cook, they'll spill their juices into the pan and get mopped up by the ricotta, which will dry out and take on a whole new texture as it bakes, while the seeds turn crunchy and fragrant. Swap the ricotta for tofu slices for an easy vegan substitute and serve it with a salad and garlic bread for a delicious meal, or load the mix onto pesto pasta for some comfort-food heaven. Because the tomatoes are roasted so well, it's less important here that they're perfectly ripe or in season.

Preheat the oven to 180°C (350°F) fan-forced. Line a large baking dish with baking paper.

Evenly spread the ricotta wedges and tomato in the dish – don't worry if they are nestled closely to each other. Drizzle over the olive oil and honey, aiming to coat as much of the ricotta and tomato as you can.

Combine the seeds, salt and some cracked black pepper in a small bowl then scatter the mixture over the ricotta and tomato. Transfer to the oven and bake for at least 1 hour or until the ricotta is starting to brown and the tomato is beginning to shrivel. Remove from the oven and drizzle over a little extra olive oil and the balsamic vinegar, and scatter with the oregano or basil. Serve warm or at room temperature, alongside some crusty bread. *

Tomato & haloumi galette

Serves 4–6

600 g (1 lb 5 oz) tomatoes (mix of colours and sizes if possible), sliced (or halved if using cherry tomatoes)

1 tsp salt

200 g (7 oz) toum (Lebanese garlic dip)

250 g (9 oz) haloumi, sliced into 5 mm (¼ in) thick slabs

2 tsp za'atar

1 tsp fennel seeds

1 egg, beaten

Simple puff pastry

150 g (5½ oz) salted cold butter, cut into cubes

260 g (1¾ cups) plain (all-purpose) flour, plus extra if needed and for dusting

½ tsp salt

80 ml (⅓ cup) ice-cold water, plus extra if needed

To serve

handful of oregano and basil leaves

olive oil

extra za'atar

Swaps

Vegan – simple puff pastry: store-bought vegan puff pastry; omit the haloumi or use vegan cheese, caramelised onions or roasted eggplant (aubergine) slices

Toum – 80 g (⅓ cup) garlicky aioli or 60 ml (¼ cup) olive oil blended with 3 garlic cloves and a pinch of salt

In this Middle Eastern–inspired galette, toum and za'atar combine beautifully with haloumi and tomato, encased in an easy homemade puff pastry. The tomato hides all these secret additions, so when you eat it there are heaps of unexpected flavours and textures that make it a delight to eat. It's a perfect vegetarian main or addition to a spread. It can be made ahead and eaten at room temperature, and it's pretty sturdy too, so can be easily transported to the park for a picnic.

To make the pastry, place the butter, flour and salt in a large bowl and use your fingers to rub the butter into the flour until well distributed but with some large chunks remaining. This can also be done in a food processor using the pulse function. Add the ice-cold water and bring the dough into a rough ball with your hands, working it just enough so that it smooshes together, adding a little extra water or flour as needed.

Transfer the dough to a lightly floured work surface and roll it out to a large square, about 2 mm (⅛ in) thick. Fold the dough over itself a few times to form a rough cube (this creates layers of pastry, which will help it puff up when cooked). Wrap the pastry in a clean tea towel or plastic wrap and set aside in the fridge for about 1 hour, until very firm. You can make the dough up to 2 days ahead.

Meanwhile, transfer the tomato to a colander set over a large bowl. Sprinkle over the salt, toss gently to combine and leave to drain for 15–20 minutes – this will prevent your galette having a soggy bottom.

Once your dough is firm, preheat the oven to 200°C (400°F) fan-forced. Line a large baking tray with baking paper.

Roll out the pastry on a lightly floured work surface to a 45 cm (18 in) large circle. Gently roll it up onto the rolling pin, then unroll onto the prepared tray. Don't worry if the pastry is bigger than the tray, as you'll fold in the edges.

Spread the toum across the centre of the pastry, leaving a 5 cm (2 in) border. Place the haloumi on top and sprinkle with the za'atar and fennel seeds. Give the tomato a gentle toss to extract any final liquid, then arrange on top of the haloumi. Fold over the pastry edge to form a galette and brush with the beaten egg. Transfer to the oven and bake for 25–35 minutes, until the crust is deep golden brown. Serve warm or at room temperature, topped with oregano and basil leaves, a drizzle of olive oil and a sprinkling of za'atar. ✳

Polenta pikelets with blistered tomatoes & corn cream

Serves 4–6

150 g (1 cup) polenta

1 tsp baking powder

75 g (½ cup) self-raising flour

½ tsp salt

250 ml (1 cup) buttermilk

1 heaped tsp dijon mustard

3 spring onions (scallions), finely chopped

2 eggs

vegetable oil, for shallow-frying

Blistered tomatoes

700 g (1 lb 9 oz) tomatoes (any variety or a mix), quartered or halved if small

2 garlic cloves, sliced

2 tbsp olive oil, plus extra for drizzling

salt and pepper

2 handfuls of basil leaves

Corn cream

1 sweetcorn cob, husks and silks removed, kernels stripped

100 g (3½ oz) sour cream

6–8 basil leaves

½ tsp salt

2 tsp white wine vinegar

2 tbsp olive oil

Swaps

Vegan – buttermilk: plant-based milk mixed with 1 tbsp lemon juice; eggs: flax or chia eggs

Gluten free – self-raising flour: cornflour (corn starch)

Tomatoes, corn and basil are a luscious summer trio that complement each other beautifully. This dish was conceived as part of a brunch spread, but the elements themselves are very versatile, so feel free to get creative with them. Add some avocado or salad greens to the tomatoes, or if you'd like more protein, serve alongside a poached or fried egg, haloumi or some crispy chickpeas. I like to use a colourful mix of tomatoes here, including cherry tomatoes, but just use whatever you can get your hands on.

Preheat the oven to 220°C (430°F) fan-forced.

To make the blistered tomatoes, place the tomato and garlic on a baking tray, drizzle with the olive oil, sprinkle with a generous pinch of salt and pepper and toss to combine, ensuring everything is well coated in the oil. Roast for 15–20 minutes, until the tomato is beginning to blister and shrivel. Remove from the oven and allow to cool for a few minutes. Toss through the basil leaves.

Meanwhile, create the corn cream by blitzing the ingredients in a blender to form a thick, silky consistency.

Stir the polenta, baking powder, flour and salt together in a large bowl. Add the remaining ingredients except the oil and whisk to combine well.

Heat a glug of vegetable oil in a large frying pan over medium heat. Once the oil is very hot, add 2 tablespoons of the batter to the pan and cook a 'test' pikelet to get a feel for how it spreads and cooks. Cook the pikelets, 2–4 at a time (depending on the size of your pan), for 2 minutes each side or until golden brown. I like them quite small, about 6 cm (2½ in) in diameter. The batter should make 12–15 pikelets at this size.

Plate up 2–3 pikelets per serve and top with the blistered tomato mixture. Drizzle over some corn cream and finish with a little extra olive oil and flaky salt. *

Fresh tomato sauce with fancy floral pappardelle

Serves 4–6

500 g (1 lb 2 oz) 00 flour, plus extra for dusting

5 eggs

2 tbsp olive oil

2 handfuls of edible flowers and herb leaves (parsley, thyme, sage, basil, marigolds and nasturtiums are all nice choices)

grated parmesan, burrata or double-thickened (dollop) cream, to serve (optional)

Fresh tomato sauce

125 ml (½ cup) olive oil, plus extra for drizzling

8–10 garlic cloves, thinly sliced or minced

2 tbsp tomato paste (concentrated purée)

1.5 kg (3 lb 5 oz) tomatoes (any variety), roughly chopped or blitzed in a food processor

1–2 tsp sea salt

2–3 tsp sugar

½ bunch of basil, leaves picked, plus extra to serve

Swaps

Vegan – eggs: 250 ml (1 cup) of warm water (follow the same method to make the pasta)

Basil leaves – 1 tsp dried basil, added with the garlic

Tomatoes – 3 x 400 g (14 oz) tins good-quality tomatoes

When we were kids my dad called his Napolitana sauce 'Scrine Penicillin'. Pasta with tomato sauce was so dearly adored by us all, I think we ate it about twice a week. The smell of onions, garlic and oregano simmering on the stove always makes me think of him, cooking in a sarong, belting out some Dylan in the kitchen as he goes. This version is simpler than Dad's, without any of his go-to herbs and aromatics. I've come to love its simplicity, which makes the tomatoes the star, but it is ripe for your own additions. It does include an unholy amount of garlic, which I know my dad will appreciate. Unlike most fresh tomato sauces, there's no need to deseed or peel the tomatoes, although you can if you're averse to their slight bitterness.

Pressing edible flowers and herbs into your pasta sheets is a lovely little touch that makes this simple meal feel really special. Just use whatever you have growing in the garden. Of course it isn't essential, and you could replace the homemade pasta with some good-quality stuff from the shops.

Start by preparing the pasta dough. Tip the flour onto a clean work surface (or into a large bowl) and create a large well in the centre. Crack the eggs in, then gently use a fork to whisk the eggs and gradually bring in the flour from the sides to create a thick paste. Once the mixture is dough-like, add the olive oil and start using your hands to knead it together. Knead for 5–8 minutes, until the dough is smooth and elastic. Cover with an upturned bowl or wrap in a clean tea towel or plastic wrap and transfer to the fridge to rest.

Meanwhile, to make the fresh tomato sauce, heat the olive oil in a large heavy-based saucepan over low heat. Add the garlic and cook gently for 2–3 minutes, until fragrant. Add the tomato paste and stir well to incorporate it into the oil. Cook for about 2 minutes, then add the tomato and any tomato juice, stirring well to combine. Leave to cook for 10–20 minutes, until the tomato has broken down into a sauce. Add 1 tsp of the salt, 2 tsp of the sugar and 500 ml (2 cups) of water and leave the sauce to bubble away over very low heat, for at least 30 minutes, and up to 2 hours. If cooking for longer, add a splash more water to prevent the sauce from becoming too thick. The sauce is ready when it has deepened in colour to a luscious red. Taste and add some extra sugar and another generous sprinkle of salt, to taste. Don't be afraid of salt here, it's essential for bringing out the tomato flavour, so if unsure, add a little more. If you have one, use a stick blender to pulse the sauce a few times to crush up some of the tomato skins and seeds, though I like to keep some of it a bit chunkier. Don't worry about blitzing the sauce if you don't have a stick blender, it'll still be great as is. →

As the sauce cooks, roll out the dough. Divide the dough into smaller portions and roll each portion through a pasta machine (or use a rolling pin) to the sixth setting or until 1 mm (1/16 in) thick. Lay each sheet on your work surface as you finish rolling it and scatter one half of each sheet with edible flower petals and herbs, removing any stems that might tear the dough. Carefully fold the empty half of each pasta sheet over the flowers and herbs and run the sheets through the pasta machine again, starting back at the third notch and rolling to the fifth or sixth notch. Dust well with flour, then individually fold up the sheets and slice into 2–3 mm (1/8 in) wide pappardelle. Gently transfer the pappardelle to a drying rack (a coat hanger or clothes drying rack work well), or dust well with flour and spread across your work surface. Allow the pasta to dry for at least 20 minutes, or up to a few hours until you're ready to serve.

Bring a large saucepan of very salty water to the boil. Cook the pappardelle in two batches, gently stirring with a wooden spoon, for 3–4 minutes, until almost al dente. Use tongs to transfer the almost-cooked pappardelle to the tomato sauce, then add 250 ml (1 cup) of the pasta cooking water and stir very gently to coat the pappardelle in the sauce. Add the basil leaves and cook for a final minute.

Divide the pasta and sauce among bowls and drizzle with a little olive oil. Scatter over a few basil leaves and serve alongside some grated parmesan, if you like, or a blob of burrata or double-thickened cream for a bit of extra luxury. ✳

Spiced tomato, eggplant & lentil soup

Serves 4–6 · Vegan · Gluten Free

60 ml (¼ cup) olive oil, plus extra
for drizzling

1 eggplant (aubergine), diced into
1 cm (½ in) cubes

1 large onion, diced

1 carrot, diced

500 g (1 lb 2 oz) tomatoes, diced

100 g (3½ oz) tomato paste
(concentrated purée)

1 tbsp harissa paste, plus extra
if desired

4 garlic cloves, minced

40 g (1½ oz) ginger, peeled and grated
or minced

2 tsp ground cumin

2 tsp ground coriander

½ tsp ground cinnamon

375 g (1½ cups) split red lentils

1.5 litres (6 cups) vegetable stock

2 bay leaves

1–2 tbsp freshly squeezed lemon juice

salt and pepper

natural yoghurt or coconut yoghurt,
to serve

parsley, dill or mint leaves, to serve

Swaps

*Eggplant (aubergine) or carrot –
capsicum (bell pepper), zucchini
(courgette), celery, mushrooms
or fennel*

*Fresh tomatoes – 1 x 400 g (14 oz)
tin tomatoes*

Some variation of tomato and lentil soup is my go-to meal when I feel like something really nourishing, but cheap and easy. This one is beautifully fragrant and comforting, thanks to the Moroccan spices and harissa, which complement the tomato base of the soup beautifully, while creamy eggplant provides a lovely texture and a little more depth. Serve this soup alongside some flatbread, topped with yoghurt and fresh herbs for a beautiful finish. You could reduce the amount of liquid and serve this dish as more of a stew, atop some pearl barley or rice pilaf.

Heat the olive oil in a large heavy-based saucepan over medium heat. Add the eggplant, onion, carrot and tomato and cook, stirring frequently, for about 15 minutes, until the eggplant is soft and the tomato has broken down.

Add the tomato and harissa pastes, garlic, ginger and spices to the vegetables and stir well to combine. Cook, stirring frequently, for 3–5 minutes, then add the lentils, vegetable stock and bay leaves. Stir the mixture really well, then bring to a slow simmer, cover with the lid and cook for 15–25 minutes, until the lentils are soft.

When the soup is ready, add 250 ml (1 cup) of water if you prefer a more liquidy soup. Finish with the lemon juice and some salt and pepper, then taste and adjust the salt or harissa to your liking.

Before serving you can use a stick blender to blend the soup if you prefer a smooth consistency, or just blitz it a little to create a creamier texture. Serve the soup in bowls topped with a swirl of yoghurt, olive oil and a few fresh herbs. ✳

Zucchini

A few zucchini can go a really long way, and they're such a versatile ingredient. Because of this, they are always included in my weekly shop, usually without any particular plans for them. Zucchini stars in these recipes in all its glorious states: raw, charred, roasted, simmered and sneakily hidden in a whopping big cake. The flavour of zucchini itself is subtle, making it a perfect bulker to stretch meals or pack in some extra vegetables, but when cooked down until jammy, or roasted until golden, its subtle flavour develops and might surprise you.

With Marissa, Theo, Lachlan, Nat and Abe

Describe your household?

Cavan Street is Nat, Lachlan and dogs Ripley and Scully in Mango Home, and Abe, Marissa, Theo and dog Squish in Watermelon Home. We share a suburban block across two houses. It's a co-housing arrangement that for us is a really deliberate and long-term decision to live this way. Coming together in this arrangement allowed us to stay in the inner city in a beautiful home, not subject to the whims of a landlord. Our home gives us a stable base to plan our lives and to practise collective skills for living in our anarcho-communist utopian future.

Do you share food as a household?

Yes! Right now, we have two shared dinners each week, where one household cooks for everyone. We also share a lot of morning teas and treats together on the deck at Mango Home. When all the grown-ups lived together in Watermelon Home, we shared food a lot. Abe and Marissa could not have survived their postpartum periods without Lachlan and Nat; they cooked countless delicious meals and just generally kept the household going. Then and now, washing up is often the best part of our days because we all pitch in and talk together – even Theo, who stands on the 'helping tower' and helps rinse things.

What's your favourite way to cook/eat zucchini?

Our favourite ways to eat zucchini (homegrown, when we're lucky!) include chargrilled on the barbecue, in a salad with haloumi and asparagus (see *The Shared Table* by Clare Scrine!), or diced and braised with onions and dressed with yoghurt, lemon and garlic (see *Falastin* by Sami Tamimi and Tara Wigley).

What do you love about living in a share house?

At their best, share houses and co-living can be an educative and nourishing way to practise the skills for more collective and more caring ways of living together, for being more responsive, engaged and entangled in our communities in ways that we hope make futures worth having, more possible. It's made us better at communication, community care and organising. The barriers we've experienced in forming this co-housing arrangement have brought into sharper relief the structural, financial, political and spatial barriers that make alternative family and kinship more difficult than they should be, and that prioritise heteronormative and colonial-capitalist modes of living. Also we just really like each other a whole lot.

What gives you and your housemates hope for a better world?

We're not sure there's hope to be had – anthropologist Anna Tsing tells us we are 'confront[ing] the condition of trouble without end'. As white settlers in this place, figuring out how to help heal and repair the harm we've caused, and support the conditions of life for others, among escalating, compounding and uneven crises, is the best we've got just now. We're not hopeful, but we're always inspired by love, joy and solidarity in these struggles. *

Charred zucchini & haloumi with pearl barley & honey

Serves 4–6 as a main, or 6–8 as a side

3 large zucchini (courgettes), halved crossways and sliced into 5 mm (¼ in) thick strips

olive oil, for drizzling

juice of 1 lemon (about 2 tbsp)

salt and pepper

220 g (1 cup) pearl barley

750 ml (3 cups) hot vegetable stock

½ large red onion, thinly sliced

2 tbsp red wine vinegar

250 g (9 oz) haloumi, sliced into 1 cm (½ in) thick slabs

3 tbsp honey

handful of mint, dill and/or parsley leaves, roughly torn or chopped

Swaps

Gluten free – pearl barley: quinoa or brown rice

Vegan – haloumi: grilled tofu, mushrooms, capsicums (bell peppers) or tomatoes; honey: maple syrup

Zucchini (courgettes) – mushrooms, tomatoes, capsicums (bell peppers) or eggplants (aubergines)

Zucchini cooked on a scorching barbecue or in a chargrill pan until charred and smoky, then coated in lemon juice, olive oil and seasoning has become a recent obsession of mine. If you haven't tried it already, you absolutely must give it a go. This warm salad can be served as I have here, with individual elements piled separately, or you can toss it all together. Some toasted nuts like pistachios or walnuts would make lovely additions, as would some extra grilled vegetables such as mushrooms or capsicums. Honey finishes everything off with a sticky sweetness that complements the salty haloumi and tangy onions.

Heat a large chargrill pan or barbecue flat plate until screaming hot. Add the zucchini strips (do this in batches if cooking in a chargrill pan) and drizzle with a little olive oil. Cook the zucchini for 5 minutes each side or until charred and blackened in parts. Transfer to a plate, drizzle with a little more oil and squeeze over the lemon juice. Season well with salt and pepper and set aside.

Meanwhile, combine the pearl barley and vegetable stock in a saucepan and bring to the boil. Reduce the heat to a simmer and cook for about 30 minutes, until the stock has evaporated and the barley is tender.

Toss the red onion and red wine vinegar together in a bowl and season with salt and pepper. Set aside until ready to serve.

Once everything is almost ready, place the haloumi in the chargrill pan or on the barbecue with a drizzle of olive oil. Cook over medium–high heat for 2 minutes each side or until golden.

Assemble the dish by scooping the pearl barley onto a serving plate. Place the charred zucchini, onion and haloumi on top, then drizzle everything with the honey. Finish with the herb leaves and serve warm. Leftovers will keep well for a couple of days in an airtight container in the fridge, and can be served cold or at room temperature. ✳

Shredded zucchini & vermicelli noodle salad

Serves 4–6 as a main or 6–8 as a side · Vegan

3–4 zucchini (courgettes), shredded into noodles

2 carrots, shredded into noodles

salt

200 g (7 oz) vermicelli noodles

4–5 radishes, halved and thinly sliced

2 green apples, sliced or shredded into matchsticks

5 spring onions (scallions), thinly sliced

small bunch of coriander (cilantro), leaves roughly chopped

small bunch of mint or Vietnamese mint, leaves roughly chopped

40 g (1½ oz) crispy fried shallots

15–20 mini vegan spring rolls, cooked according to the packet instructions and halved

Nuoc cham dressing

60 ml (¼ cup) vegan fish sauce

2 tbsp rice wine vinegar

juice of 1 large lime (1–2 tbsp)

2 tbsp brown sugar

1 garlic clove, finely grated

pinch of chilli flakes (or more, to taste)

Swaps

Gluten free – spring rolls: cooked tofu or plant-based meat

Green apple – green mango or green papaya

Spring rolls – cooked crispy tofu or veggie sausages

Zucchini (courgettes) – cucumber

This salad is super zingy and packed with fresh, delicious veggies and herbs. While the zucchini noodles add bulk, finely chopped apple adds a nice tart sweetness and the hot, crispy spring rolls finish things off deliciously and make it feel more substantial. I use a mandoline to thinly slice the vegetables and then I cut them into wide 'noodles', but you can also just peel them with a vegetable peeler, use a spiraliser or thinly slice them into matchsticks.

Combine the shredded veggies in a colander and season with a couple of teaspoons of salt. Toss well to ensure that the salt is evenly distributed, then set aside for 5 minutes. Rinse the veg well and gently toss to dry.

Meanwhile, cook the vermicelli in boiling water for 2 minutes or until just cooked through. Drain and rinse under cold water to prevent overcooking.

Prepare the dressing by whisking the ingredients together in a small bowl. Taste and adjust the flavour balance if necessary.

Place the zucchini, carrot, noodles, radish, apple, spring onion and most of the herbs in a serving bowl. Add the dressing and toss well to combine, then scatter with the crispy fried shallots and remaining herbs. Serve immediately, topped with the halved spring rolls. ✻

Creamy mint & zucchini ribbon pasta

Serves 5–6

500 g (1 lb 2 oz) long pasta, such as linguine or spaghetti

80 ml (⅓ cup) olive oil

4 zucchini (courgettes), cut into long thin ribbons (this can be done quickly with the help of a spiraliser, mandoline or vegetable peeler)

4 spring onions (scallions), cut in half crossways, then into long strips

4 garlic cloves, minced

zest of ½ lemon and juice of 1 lemon

salt and pepper

300 ml (10 fl oz) light pouring cream

½ bunch mint, leaves picked and chopped, plus extra to serve

100 g (3½ oz) baby spinach leaves

50 g (½ cup) grated parmesan, plus extra to serve

Swaps

Zucchini (courgettes) – ribboned asparagus, kale, broccolini or yellow (pattypan) squash

With a simple ingredients list and a very short cooking time, the hardest part of this recipe is cutting up the zucchini and spring onions into their long strands. Everything comes together quickly, but there's something special about the combination of rich and fresh that makes this pasta super moreish. The zucchini ribbons and spring onions will cook down enormously and almost get lost in the pasta as it all comes together, but their subtle flavour perfumes the whole dish.

Cook the pasta in a large saucepan of heavily salted boiling water until al dente.

Meanwhile, heat the olive oil in a large frying pan over medium heat. Add the zucchini and spring onion and increase the heat to high. Cook, tossing occasionally, for 5–8 minutes, until the vegetables have sweated out a lot of their liquid.

Add the garlic and lemon zest to the vegetables, along with a generous sprinkle of salt and pepper. Reduce the heat to medium and cook for 1–2 minutes, then pour in the cream, add the mint, spinach and lemon juice and stir well to wilt the leaves.

Use tongs to drag the pasta from the pan into the sauce, along with about 125 ml (½ cup) of the pasta cooking water.

Sprinkle over the parmesan, then use the tongs to combine everything together, ensuring that the pasta is well coated in the creamy sauce. Add a little extra pasta water if needed. Finish the pasta with some extra seasoning, and serve topped with extra mint leaves and grated parmesan, and plenty of black pepper. *

Zucchini & mozzarella ratatouille with gremolata

Serves 4–6 · Gluten Free

60 ml (¼ cup) olive oil, plus extra
for drizzling

1 onion, finely diced

5 garlic cloves, thinly sliced

2 x 400 g (14 oz) tins crushed
tomatoes

1 tsp dried or fresh oregano

2 tsp brown sugar

1 tbsp balsamic vinegar

salt and pepper

3–4 zucchini (courgettes), sliced into
2 mm (⅛ in) thick rounds

200 g (7 oz) ball of mozzarella,
thinly sliced

Gremolata

80 g (½ cup) almonds, toasted and
roughly chopped

zest and juice of 1 small lemon

60 ml (¼ cup) olive oil

salt and pepper

½ bunch of basil, leaves roughly
chopped

Swaps

*Vegan – mozzarella: roasted eggplant
(aubergine) slices, cooked potato
slices or vegan cheese*

*Almonds – toasted walnuts or
pumpkin seeds (pepitas)*

*Zucchini (courgettes) – eggplant,
mushrooms, capsicum (bell pepper)
or fennel*

This dish makes a beautiful centrepiece to a shared meal or a great addition to a potluck dinner and, despite its simplicity, I think it really makes the zucchini shine. I love serving it alongside garlic bread and a simple leafy salad. If you have a good ovenproof frying pan, this is a great one-pan meal.

Heat the olive oil in an ovenproof frying pan over medium heat. Add the onion and cook, stirring frequently, for 10 minutes or until starting to brown. Add the garlic and cook for 2 minutes or until fragrant, then add the tomatoes and oregano and cook, stirring well, for 5 minutes. Add the brown sugar, vinegar and some salt and pepper, and stir well to combine. Add a splash of water, then reduce the heat to a gentle simmer and cook for 10–15 minutes, until very thick and rich.

Meanwhile, preheat the oven to 200°C (400°F) fan-forced.

Toss the zucchini and mozzarella in a generous drizzle of olive oil. Season with salt and pepper.

Take the pan off the heat, check the seasoning and adjust if necessary. Starting at the outer edge, arrange the zucchini in concentric circles, overlapping each slice by about a third and placing at an angle so they nestle in the sauce. Add a slice of mozzarella every 3–4 slices of zucchini. Transfer to the oven and bake for 20–30 minutes, until the top is brown and the sauce is bubbling up through the zucchini.

Meanwhile, combine all the ingredients for the gremolata in a mortar and, using the pestle, pound for 1–2 minutes to create a chunky paste. If you don't have a mortar and pestle, simply add the ingredients, except the juice and oil, to a large chopping board and chop until well combined. Add to a bowl and stir through the juice and oil. Taste the gremolata and adjust the seasoning if necessary. Add an extra drizzle of olive oil or a tablespoon of water to loosen the gremolata to a spoonable consistency.

Serve the ratatouille fresh from the oven, dotted with the gremolata and an extra drizzle of olive oil. ✳

Roasted zucchini & butter beans with caper & pistachio dressing

Serves 4–6 · Vegan · Gluten Free

800 g (1 lb 12 oz) zucchini (courgettes), sliced into 5 mm (¼ in) thick rounds

3 x 400 g (14 oz) tins butter (lima) beans

olive oil

salt and pepper

½ bunch of cavolo nero, leaves stripped and roughly torn into bite-sized pieces

3–4 radishes, halved and thinly sliced into half moons

Caper & pistachio dressing

75 g (½ cup) shelled pistachios

2 tbsp capers, rinsed and drained

2 tbsp olive oil, plus extra if needed

1 garlic clove, peeled

juice of 1 lemon (about 2 tbsp)

2 tbsp butter bean soaking liquid from the tin

½ bunch of flat-leaf parsley, leaves picked

Swaps

Cavolo nero – mixed salad greens, rocket (arugula) or shredded silverbeet (Swiss chard) (refrain from massaging the leaves if using another leafy green)

Most of the work here happens in the oven, making it a hands-off and pretty speedy dish. The dressing on this warm salad is incredible, and I recommend doubling the quantity to serve on roast vegetables, in sandwiches and breakfasts for the rest of the week. Because the roasted beans and zucchini dry out so much in the oven, the dressing soaks in and flavours the entire dish beautifully. This dish pairs really well with loads of other cuisines and makes a great potluck plate or veggie addition to a bigger spread. Serve it alongside veggie sausages with some hummus, or haloumi and tzatziki for a lovely summer meal.

Preheat the oven to 200°C (400°F) fan-forced.

To prepare the caper and pistachio dressing, scatter the pistachios over a baking tray and toast in the oven as it warms for 5–10 minutes, until slightly darker in colour. Tip into a bowl and set aside.

Meanwhile, arrange the zucchini slices across two large baking trays lined with baking paper, spreading them out so there's minimal overlap. Drain the butter beans, reserving 2 tablespoons of the liquid for the dressing. Pour the beans into a colander and rinse well, then shake or pat dry with a clean tea towel. It's important to remove any excess water from the beans, otherwise they'll create steam in the oven and won't become crispy. Tip the beans onto a separate baking tray lined with baking paper, spreading them out as much as possible. Drizzle the zucchini and beans with some olive oil and sprinkle with a little salt and pepper. Transfer all three trays to the oven and roast for 30–40 minutes, checking and turning the zucchini and beans over halfway through cooking. The zucchini are ready when they are golden and considerably shrivelled; the beans when most of them have popped open and crisped up at the edges. Once cooked, remove the trays from the oven and leave to cool a little.

Blitz the pistachios and remaining dressing ingredients except the parsley in a food processor or blender, until you have a thick paste, adding a little extra olive oil or water to get things moving if necessary. Add the parsley and pulse until just combined, adding another splash of oil or water if needed.

Place the cavolo nero in a serving bowl and drizzle with a spoonful of the dressing. Use your hands to massage the dressing into the leaves, until lightly softened. Add the warm zucchini and crispy butter beans and toss gently to combine. Spoon over the remaining dressing and scatter over the radish. Drizzle with a little extra olive oil and serve. ✳

Chocolate & zucchini cake with luscious cream-cheese icing

Serves 10–12

3 eggs

150 g (5½ oz) sour cream

250 ml (1 cup) vegetable oil (or other neutral oil)

170 ml (⅔ cup) black coffee, cooled

2 tsp vanilla extract

270 g (2 cups) finely grated zucchini (courgette) (from 2–3 zucchini)

325 g (1¾ cups) brown sugar

1 tsp salt

300 g (2 cups) self-raising flour

½ tsp bicarbonate of soda (baking soda)

90 g (¾ cup) Dutch-processed cocoa powder

Cream-cheese icing

375 g (3 cups) icing (confectioners') sugar

85 g (⅔ cup) good-quality cocoa powder

150 g (5½ oz) salted butter, at room temperature

375 g (13 oz) cream cheese, at room temperature

To fill and top

250 ml (1 cup) double-thickened (dollop) cream

400 g (14 oz) cherries and mixed berries

Swaps

Cherries and berries – poached pears, or fresh plums or figs

Coffee – hot water

I promise you can't actually see, taste or smell the zucchini in this cake. Instead, the vegetable adds moisture and helps to create a really beautiful classic chocolate cake that makes a perfect celebration centrepiece when loaded up with berries and slathered in the best icing ever. It's easy to handle, including to slice and fill with extra icing, and will keep fresh for days in the fridge. Coffee adds a depth of flavour and additional moisture to the batter, but you won't taste it unless you make an extra-strong cup.

Preheat the oven to 170°C (340°F) fan-forced. Line two 25–30 cm (10–12 in) springform cake tins with baking paper.

In a large bowl, whisk together the eggs, sour cream, vegetable oil, cooled coffee and vanilla until well combined and a little frothy. Add the zucchini and stir well to combine. In a separate large bowl, combine the sugar, salt, flour, bicarbonate of soda and cocoa powder.

Add the wet ingredients to the dry ingredients and stir gently until just combined, ensuring you scrape right to the bottom of the bowl to mix well. Distribute the mixture evenly between the two prepared tins, then transfer to the oven and bake for 25–35 minutes, until a skewer inserted into the centre of each cake comes out mostly clean. It's important not to overcook the cakes, so keep a close eye on them. Once cooked, remove from the oven and leave to cool for a few minutes, then snap off the sides of the tins and leave to cool completely.

Meanwhile, prepare the cream-cheese icing. Sift and combine the icing sugar and cocoa powder in a bowl and set aside. In a separate larger bowl, beat the butter with electric beaters until light and fluffy. Add the cream cheese and beat until incorporated and smooth. Add the icing sugar mixture in two batches, beating well to combine after each addition.

Place one of the cakes on a serving stand or plate. Top with a thin layer of icing, using the back of a spoon or a knife to spread and swirl the icing so that it's flat and evenly distributed. Spread the cream over the top, then arrange about half the berries over that. Carefully add a thin layer of icing to the remaining cake, then place, icing side down, on top of the berries, pressing gently to ensure it sits flat. Top the cake generously with the remaining icing, spreading it all around the cake with a flat spatula or spreader. Top with the remaining berries and serve. *

Feast suggestions

Celebration meal for the masses

Finger foods

Acknowledgements

Firstly, to the crew at Smith Street Books. Paul McNally, I don't think I would have written a second cookbook without your nudging. Now that it's done, I'm so glad it exists. Thanks for bringing book two to life. Lucy Heaver, thank you for all the work you've poured into every one of these pages, you have made it so wonderful. Having you to turn to made this process far less daunting and I'm so appreciative of your keen eye.

Shooting a cookbook out of a share-house kitchen in the middle of a heatwave and a pandemic was far from easy, but I was so lucky to do it with a dream team. Yaseera, you probably had no idea what you were signing yourself up for when I asked you to photograph this book. Thank you for coming along for the ride and rolling with all my chaos so beautifully. Your endless calm professionalism, with a sprinkling of wry humour just when it's needed, was so appreciated on set. I couldn't love the photos in this book any more, and I hope you feel proud. Issy, my oldest friend and most trusted collaborator. Thank you for your endless determination and dedication to making this thing beautiful and not letting me get impatient and say 'fuck it' too much. Working alongside you feels like home and no matter where our lives take us, I hope that never changes. Sav, across continents, I'm so glad we were able to work together again for another book. Thank you for your focused time, skill and energy into turning my words and Yaseera's beautiful images into the most wonderfully considered and professional book.

To all the mates who helped during the truly chaotic two weeks we shot this book, and all the shopping, cleaning and meltdown-soothing labour surrounding it. Thank you Bam, Al, Suf, Liv, Anna Z, Emerald, Harriet and Fin. In very on-brand fashion, I bit off far more than I could chew during those weeks and having at least one of you around each day doing the dishes, grabbing the forgotten groceries and passing round the waters made the whole process possible.

A particularly special shout-out to Anna R, Jackson and Maeve, who between them did the lion's share of this work, day in and day out. Thank you for making our shoot feel like a big team project, having you all around made things so much more fun. Thanks to each of you too, for your endless feedback and idea bouncing during the last year or so. How damn lucky am I to call each of you my friends.

Thank you to my eternally patient and present housemates, Fynn, Maeve (you get two shout-outs!), Isy and Isha. Thank you for letting me turn our house into a photography studio and kindly dealing with all the mess, people, noise and stress that came with it. Thank you for testing so many of these recipes and providing your feedback. And most of all, thanks for being amazing people to live alongside every single day.

To my family. Mum and Dad, Judy and Michael, thank you for your support and care. How bloody privileged I feel to have two parents and two bonus parental figures whose pride and love I carry with me every day. To my siblings Jack, Elly and Hannah. I love you all so deeply and admire so keenly how you all live your lives. Thank you especially to Elly, who came to Brisbane to help me with the shoots only to get pinged as a close contact and spend the week in isolation. Thanks, El also for all your recipe testing and feedback, all of which resulted in improvements to this book.

Jackson, you get another special one. Thank you for being my endless collaborator, a patient voice, a proofreader and dishes-doer. I don't think either of these books would have come to life without your encouragement and Big Producer Energy. I love you, and I love sharing life with you.

In hindsight, making a book in the middle of a pandemic, never mind in 16 different locations and households, was a bonkers thing to do. Thank you to all the houses who welcomed us into your lives for a bit, and for letting me use your images and words to make up this book. I hope these pages serve as a little time capsule into a moment in your lives that can hold some meaning for you for many years to come. I feel very privileged to have been allowed into your homes. Thanks for building them and caring for them.

Dozens of people tested recipes for this book and there are too many to name here. But please know that I read each one of your comments and pieces of feedback, and these recipes are far better because of it. Thank you so much.

'I'm so grateful for the wonderful local makers who lent us their work to include in these photographs. They're all amazing and you should check them out. Thank you so much Anna Markey (@a_cermanics), Wendy Ma (@kamoji.ceramics), Jennifer Hillhouse, (@jennifer.hillhouse), Mirika Guffin (@milk.ceramics) and Five Mile Radius (@five_mile_radius).'

That's probably enough for now, except to say thanks too, to you, the reader. I hope this book brings you some nice times in the kitchen, or inspires some good catch-ups with friends, family or housemates. ✱

—Clare

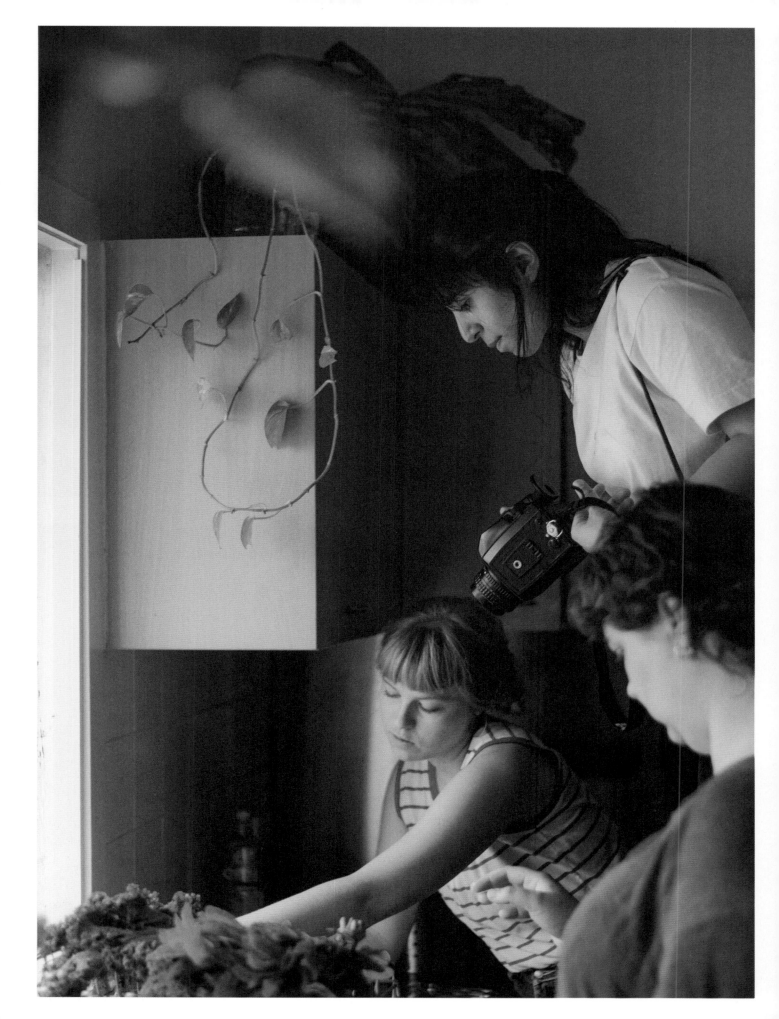

Index

Published in 2022 by Smith Street Books
Naarm | Melbourne | Australia
smithstreetbooks.com

ISBN: 978-1-9227-5412-7 (Flexi edition)
ISBN: 978-1-9224-1789-3 (Hardback edition)

Publisher: Paul McNally

Senior editor: Lucy Heaver, Tusk Studio

Designer: Savannah van der Niet

Cover designer: Savannah van der Niet

Photographer: Yaseera Moosa

Stylist: Issy FitzSimons Reilly

Food preparation: Clare Scrine

Typesetter: Savannah van der Niet

Proofreader: Pamela Dunne

Indexer: Helena Holmgren

Printed & bound in China by C&C Offset Printing Co., Ltd.

Book 225
10 9 8 7 6 5 4 3 2 1